CHAUCER'S
Parlement of Foules

CHAUCER'S *Parlement of Foules*

In Its Relation to Contemporary Events

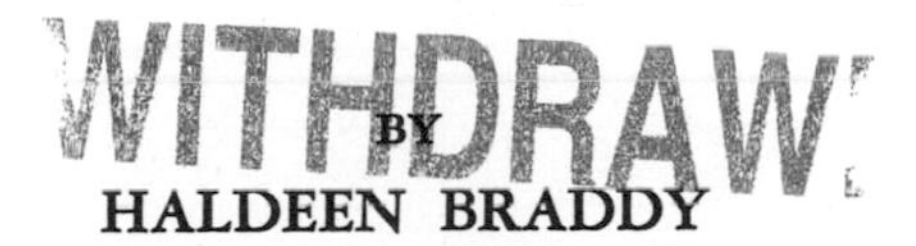

BY

HALDEEN BRADDY

[*with additional material by the author*]

1969
OCTAGON BOOKS
New York

Reprinted 1969
by special arrangement with Haldeen Braddy

OCTAGON BOOKS
A DIVISION OF FARRAR, STRAUS & GIROUX, INC.
19 Union Square West
New York, N. Y. 10003

LIBRARY OF CONGRESS CATALOG CARD NUMBER: 78-84176

Printed in U.S.A. by
NOBLE OFFSET PRINTERS, INC.
NEW YORK 3, N. Y.

TO

HASKELL AND FRANCES HATFIELD

PREFACE TO THE OCTAGON EDITION

Early in the 'thirties I earned a Ph.D. in English at New York University, studying mainly under two distinguished medievalists, Professors Carleton Brown, now deceased, and Margaret Schlauch, most recently of the University of Warsaw. The centennial celebration of the founding of New York University came in 1932, when I completed my doctoral dissertation, on Chaucer. Written under the direction of Professor Brown, this work was issued incidental to that celebration as *Chaucer's "Parlement of Foules" in Its Relation to Contemporary Events,* being originally published by the Oxford University Press as the second section of the book *Three Chaucer Studies* (London and New York, 1932). The present edition contains important addenda, especially in those sections labeled Introduction and The Problem Since 1932.

Long out of print, my publication on Chaucer's "Parlement" is now issued individually by Octagon Books, in response to inquiries by numerous graduate students. Several present-day scholars also expressed an interest in having this work made available anew. In particular, Dr. Alan Gunn, an eminent Southwestern medievalist, repeatedly urged me to have it reprinted. On his own initiative, Dr. Gunn recommended its republication, corresponding to this end with the original publishers as well as with Mr. Henry Schlanger, of Octagon Books. The additional materials appearing here represent the outcome of my probings into and cogitations upon this "superproblem" of medievalist scholarship.

My research inquiries were facilitated through a grant by The University of Texas at El Paso from the Committee on Organized Research, directed by Dean E. B. Coleman. In June, 1967, I resumed my readings in the British Museum. My brief sojourn in London was underwritten in part from a travel fund created for my use. This fund resulted from the generosity of my two friends, Dr. Haskell Doke Hatfield and his wife, Frances Hatfield. It is to these two sponsors of my research that this edition is gratefully dedicated.

A more recent allotment in 1968 afforded me further research time. Relief from classroom duties came with a special leave. This respite from lecturing, which enabled me to continue my studies in libraries at Austin, Chicago, New Haven, New York, and elsewhere, was arranged by President Joseph M. Ray, Vice-President Robert Milton Leech, Dean Ray Small, and the Head of the English Department, Dr. John O. West. To all these champions of learning, I wish to express my sincere appreciation. My acknowledgements also must be extended to Mr. Baxter Polk, Head Librarian, and his staff of archivists, who assisted me in securing access to rare articles and books.

I further need to mention a few others, who have helped me in my labors. This group includes my technical assistants, Mr. Richard Escontrías and Miss Patricia A. Gonyea; the students of my Chaucer seminar in 1968, especially Mrs. Mary Curry; and finally the experienced assistance of my wife, Virginia Bell Braddy.

The University of Texas at El Paso
September, 1968

Haldeen Braddy

INTRODUCTION TO THE OCTAGON EDITION

Preliminary Remarks

The genesis of this study of the *Parlement of Foules* dates from graduate work that I commenced with youthful enterprise. In 1930, as a scholar aged twenty-two, I entered the English student's classical battlefield, Chaucerian scholarship. As a student in a seminar conducted by the late Professor Carleton Brown, I drew for my topic Chaucer's celebrated bird allegory. In 1931 the resulting paper appeared in *PMLA,* XLVI, 1007-19. This first version matured a year later into my doctoral dissertation, *Chaucer's "Parlement of Foules" in Its Relation to Contemporary Events,* accepted by New York University and, as already noted, published by the Oxford University Press in 1932.

The published version of 1932 included a detailed bibliography. With the object of bringing the listing up to date, I have incorporated at the end of the present work a compilation on "The Problem Since 1932." It treats the main issue in a descriptive evaluation of later research in this continually challenging field. "The Problem Since 1932" addresses itself to the restless surge and ebb of battle lines in the historic combat over the *Parlement of Foules.*

The Poet's Continental Interests

The captivating notion endures that the author of "Whan that Aprill with his shoures soote" was a nature poet *per se.* The most misleading aspect of this fallacy is its ignoring Chaucer's extensive and urbane acquaintance with Continental world capitals. He had known these cities and countries not simply as a private citizen abroad. His numerous diplomatic missions often designated his function as royal marital ambassador. The recent significant transpiration of Chaucer's mission to Navarre in 1366 affords new evidence that his services were prized as a marital envoy. His official duties kept him traveling to Latin countries and required him to stay informed on government matters similar to those involving the "commune profit" treated in Chaucer's allegory (73-84).

During his formative period as a negotiator of peace treaties or of *mariages de convenance*, the poet journeyed at least twice to Italy, in 1372-73 and 1378. Hence some degree of multilingualism would be a prerequisite to or an increment from these travels. His grasp of Italian can be, and usually is, hypothesized sufficient to have enabled the English diplomat-poet to read classical Italian writers in their native idiom. His second appointment, as emissary to Lombardy, is often construed, quite logically it appears, as evidence of his previous acquaintance with Italian. On this basis, the year 1377 hardly "seems a trifle early"[1] for passages from Boccaccio and Dante to become available for appearance in Chaucer's *Parlement*.

Neither did Chaucer as translator-poet feel restricted to local English scenes for his settings. His Continental background would not let him cast a conventionalized nature poem like the *Parlement* in

[1] Donald C. Baker, "The Parliament of Fowls," *Companion to Chaucer Studies*, ed. Beryl Rowland (Oxford, 1968), p. 363.

the pastoral English countryside. The Francophile bilingual kings, Edward III and Richard II, and their bicultural courts could be expected to savor knowingly the poet's going beyond mere regional events in England for the occasion of a historical allegory, utilizing the Continental betrothal of Richard and Marie. Noble and folk both would relish the *Parlement* as a "romance with key." The projected wedlock of this English Prince and French Princess would clearly relate to the motive of "commune profit," which nowadays so many scholars hold to be a main idea in this prothalamion. Here, as in the *Knight's Tale* (3076), the act of "parlement" leads to "advice"; in both instances too this "advice" is for the lovers to wed. The union of English and French nobility might well be expected to bring the Hundred Years' War to a halt, advancing various rival interests to the common profit of all.

The drain of the war on the London Exchequer would perturb ambitious personages at the English Court near to aging Edward III. From a partisan slant, they would expect that the King should expend his riches, not on war, but upon his favorites, in particular his mistress, Alice Perrers.

The Manly Controversy

Today my dissertation can stand without significant revision. If it were possible for me to rewrite the work, I would make a few changes in the presentation; the essential argument of my original study, however, remains the same. My interest in the *Parlement* has continued through the years. When Professor John M. Manly attacked my views in 1934, I rejoined the next year.[2] His only valid criticism, in my opinion, was a technical point; namely, that I had quoted different editions of Froissart's text, once from Buchon and once from Luce. It is thus untrue that I conjured up a new research methodology to make out my case. My act was an inadvertence; I admitted to the fault. Manly further alleged that Froissart confused the negotiations of 1377 with those of 1378 and that versions of his *Chroniques* showed him constantly "changing his mind." I replied by unearthing a new writ on Richard Stury, Chaucer's fellow ambassador, which verified the date of 1377. The document confirmed in this manner the historical report of the betrothal. The other contemporary reporters were Froissart, of course, and two other authorities.[3]

Manly adduced a document written on Christmas Eve of 1376 which omitted Marie's name. From this circumstance, he argued that she had died before the marriage negotiations of 1377 began. But in doing so, Manly ignored or forgot another *mandement* of this date which did include her name. He made no mention at all of a document (No. 1325, dated January 24, 1377) which referred to Marie by name. Moreover, it was one of the few *mandements* to be properly indexed.

It is unfortunate that a second communication of mine has not been remembered or referred to by scholars since the time of my interchanges with

[2] See the supplementary bibliography for this series of interchanges.

[3] See original text, p. 16, n. 10 and p. 18, n. 14.

Manly. Their neglect no doubt arose from my youthful oversight, for I simply failed to incorporate *Parlement of Foules* into my title: "Froissart's Account of Chaucer's Embassy in 1377," *RES,* XIV (1938), 1-5. Due to this, my second communication is practically never associated with the *Parlement.* It is not even listed in Baugh's 1968 Goldentree Bibliography. In consequence, it is necessary here to resurrect this old matter. The reason behind my treatment was to restore confidence in Froissart, because Manly challenged, not just me, but Froissart himself. To set Manly to rights, I had to seek out data on Marie's actual funeral clothing.

> Froissart's own statement in the Soubise MS. of his *Chroniques* (noted also by Manly, *ibid.,* XI, 209-13) that her death occurred shortly *after* that of Edward III (June 21, 1377) is itself a sufficient commentary on the improbability of the view that she died prior to January, 1377. And the payment on May 30, 1377, for her funeral pall may be taken as fixing approximately the date of her death (page 1).

The French Influence

More than a decade after the Manly controversy, I wrote *Chaucer and the French Poet Graunson* (1947; reprinted 1968). It relates to the present problem in the comparison it draws between Chaucer's *Parlement of Foules* and his friend Graunson's *Songe sainct Valentin.* The points of similarity are enumerated in my book, page 65.

1. Like Chaucer, Graunson has a dream vision.
2. Again like Chaucer, he is transported to a world

featuring a grand assembly of birds of every species.

3. In the *Songe* as in the *Parlement* the birds have assembled for the purpose of choosing mates.
4. In both poems the birds speak the language of courtly love.
5. Both the *Songe* and the *Parlement* conclude with all the lovers selecting mates except one bird: in Graunson it is the "faucon pelerin"; in Chaucer, it is the "formel."

In further support of *Songe* as a model for the *Parlement* one may remark that Graunson composed many poems to celebrate Saint Valentine's Day. These French verses, likewise, contain insinuations personal rather than fictional. *Le Songe* incorporates an acrostic revealing the name *Isabel* for Graunson's *amie*. Here in the verses of a known friend of Chaucer's existed a precedent for the *Parlement* being prompted by contemporary incidents and real persons. If Chaucer's "treatise" tries to reconcile true and false felicity, as R. M. Lumiansky[4] maintains, it is my contention that by true happiness the poet means human love. If religious fervor flavors the work, as Huppé and Robertson believe[5], it is my contention that this fervor is the sweet religiosity of *amour*. Chaucer's royal fowls enact the traditional roles of courtly or illicit love; I see no means of identifying either them or any of the other figures with the practice of lawful love approved by the Church.

[4] See the supplementary bibliography.

[5] *Ibid.*

If the birds represent politicians or strata of society, they only do so as these personages or classes will be affected by, or concerned in, the approaching union of Richard and Marie. Chaucer plainly means to imply that the situation may develop into more than a betrothal. Certainly one way of interpreting his closing lines, where "rede" may signify either read or advise, is to envisage him as hoping for a wedding. From this view, the *Parlement* appears as a prothalamion with its author aspiring to meet with something that will enable him to advise his patron better.

> I wok, and othere bokes tok me to,
> To reede upon, and yit I rede alwey.
> I hope, ywis, to rede so som day
> That I shal mete som thyng for to fare
> The bet, and thus to rede I nyl nat spare.

La Femme du Monde

Chaucer's penchant for realistic satire belongs to the late period of the *Canterbury Tales*. At an earlier stage, during his so-called French period, he produced courtly compliments for his patrons. One of these was a patroness at the apex of her power in 1377, namely Alice Perrers, long King Edward's paramour. It was bruited everywhere that Sir Richard Stury was one of her intimates and privy to her deepest secret dealings. In the spring of 1377 Chaucer and Stury crossed and recrossed the Channel at exactly the same dates[6] (February 13, 17 to

[6] See original text, p. 32, n. 17.

March 25) and thus no doubt together. The only conceivable interest Alice Perrers could have in France would be to end the war there. Rightly arranged, a *mariage de convenance* could accomplish exactly that. Guischard d'Angle had lately starred at negotiating grand marriages for Gaunt and York with the Spanish princesses, Constance and Isabel. When Froissart mentioned d'Angle along with Chaucer and Stury as the English emissaries in 1377, it was almost superfluous for the French writer to add that these marital ambassadors came to arrange the betrothal of Richard and Marie.

For a postscript, Alice Perrers may or may not have been the prototype of the sovereign lady of Chaucer's *Parlement*: "My rightful lady, Goddesse of Nature!" (639). Dame Alice had long exercised much influence in the affairs of Parliament, where she had enough critics and partisans to afford an historical counterpart for the debaters and dissension pictured by Chaucer in his allegory. In startling ways this woman of the world resembles "Nature." She also fits other requirements; it is likely that Chaucer owed allegiance to her patronage.[7] His house above Aldgate stood amid properties once

[7] See my article, "Chaucer and Dame Alice Perrers," *Speculum*, XXI (1946), 222-228. This woman may be the original of Chaucer's portrait of Alice of Bath. Moreover, according to a contemporary authority, one of her earlier names was Alice Chawpeneys. I intend soon to publish documentation linking her with Cecily Chaumpaigne, who in 1380 released Chaucer *"de raptu meo."* Meanwhile, the return of Gaunt and Alice Perrers to the Bad Parliament of 1377 as its leaders may be what Chaucer meant when depicting the avian assembly as being governed by the royal tercelet and Dame Nature.

owned by Alice, and she might well have given him free rental there as reward for his services.

Later in 1377 her enemies increased in number, and Parliament took action against her for growing interference in the King's business. Interpreted as a political debate, the dissension among Chaucer's fowls mirrors the turbulent parliamentary events of 1377 with astonishing clarity.

Of Stars, Poets, and Kings

Since Chaucer read works on astronomy and composed at least one treatise on the subject himself, his allusion in this bird poem to the position of the star Venus as "north-north-west" (117) has been taken by almost everybody as the poet-astronomer's own personal scientific observation. In my dissertation, on data of the eminent Harlow Shapley, I thus placed Chaucer's allusion to Venus in April, 1377. Now, I can add that Marie's recondite father, Charles le Sage, had interests in astronomy that compare with Chaucer's. In "Hat Chaucer den Kompass Gekannt und Benutzt?" Hugo Lange, the famous German scholar, delved into the library holdings of the learned King Charles of France. Arguing that "north-north-west" meant a magnetic reading from a circle of more than twenty-four parts, Lange discovered that at an early date the French king owned such an instrument. Containing a card showing thirty-two parts, this famous nautical compass bore the inscription: *"Atlas Catalane de Charles V, 1375"* (a map of Catalonia, a northern province of Spain). No doubt Chaucer knew Catalonia, as a newly discovered document depicts him traveling through nearby Navarre in 1366.[8]

Finally, in *Companion to Chaucer Studies* Donald C. Baker recently said that the *Parlement* represents a love vision with a kind of *demande d'amour* appended. Its plot requires Saint Valentine's Day, for its subject concerns *amour*. Then Baker wrote "The poem may well have been intended as a compliment, and it would be foolish to deny the possibility; in fact, Braddy's case is very tempting . . ." (p. 362 f.). To tempt the reader further, I claimed in the same book *(Companion,* p. 126) that Chaucer's locale was France, reading as a double entendre his avowal that "The note, I trowe, imaked was in Fraunce" (677). At Paris, Chaucer, as an aide in negotiating Richard's betrothal to Marie, may have seen Charles' compass in the royal palace there. The pace for parleying must have been at least as leisurely then as now; there would be time to treat of books as well as weddings. At Paris in the early spring of 1377, the ambassador Chaucer unquestionably spoke to the French king about his daughter. Charles was something of a bibliophile and savant; perhaps the two men therefore discussed sundry matters, such as a "note" generated "in Fraunce" and a fascinating new sea compass. From such materials, poems may derive; from these, I believe, came Chaucer's *Parlement*.

[8] *CLR*, ed. M. M. Crow and C. C. Olson (Oxford, 1966), p. 64. Though I have not checked, it is in contested Navarre that one might look for another suitor for Marie, as Charles V desired for French influence to remain potent there.

PREFATORY NOTE

The present study is a development of views which were outlined briefly in my paper, 'The *Parlement of Foules:* A New Proposal,' which was published in December, 1931 (*P. M. L. A.,* XLVI, 1007–19). In the six months following the printing of this paper, I have gathered some additional material bearing on the problem, and I also have opportunity here to present and discuss the evidence in fuller detail.

In publishing this study I wish to make acknowledgment of assistance which I have received in the course of my investigations: I owe an indirect debt of gratitude to Professor Frederic Duncalf, of the University of Texas, for introducing me to the material for the study of mediæval history. Miss Edith Scroggs, of London, has consulted and copied official writs for me in the Public Record Office and in the British Museum. Mr. James A. Work has more than once kindly assisted me by consulting references in the Yale University Library. To Mr. Nelson McCombs, Librarian, and Mr. H. G. Bausfield, of the Washington Square Library, I express thanks for several kindnesses rendered me in the search for rare books. To Professors Oliver Towles and P. H. Graham, of New York University, to Professor W. L. Bullock, of the University of Chicago, and to Dr. Harlow Shapley and Miss Jennie Mohr, of the Harvard College Observatory, I am grateful for a number of services recorded in their proper places. Finally, to Professor Carleton Brown, of New York University, I am under obligations not only for suggesting the subject of this investigation but also for many specific suggestions in the course of its prosecution. Without his encouragement and assistance, this study could hardly have been completed.

H. B.

CONTENTS

INTRODUCTORY

FOR more than half a century scholars have been engaged in attempts to solve the problems of Chaucer's *Parlement of Foules,* but it cannot be said that they have yet reached general agreement in interpreting it. According to the opinion of the majority, Chaucer, under the guise of allegory, was treating in this poem of actual persons and contemporary events, just as, a few years earlier, he had written the *Book of the Duchess* with reference to the death of the Duchess of Lancaster. Those who see personal allegory in the poem point to the fact that the court poets of the fourteenth century frequently employed bird and beast allegory as a literary device for dealing with political questions and personal intrigues.[1]

Of the historical interpretations of the *Parlement* which have been proposed in the attempt to discover the occasion for its composition, the view that it refers to the negotiations for the marriage of young King Richard II and Anne of Bohemia is the one which has been most persistently advocated and is still widely accepted. This theory will be taken up for detailed consideration in Chapter IV.

[1] Deschamps' *La Fiction de l'Aigle* is a satire of the court of Charles VI. (Cf. Rickert, *M. P.,* XVIII, 4.) Machault used bird-allegory in the celebration of a love match in *Le Dit de L'Alerion.* (Cf. Hoepffner's ed., *Soc. des Anc. Textes Franç.,* II, 239ff.) Froissart's *Le Temple d'Amour* is accorded a similar historical interpretation. (Cf. Brusendorff, *The Chaucer Tradition,* 158–62.)

But the attempt to explain the poem as allegorical has been vigorously challenged in recent years by some scholars. Professor Manly not only attacks the theory that the *Parlement* refers to the marriage of Richard and Anne, but he denies that Chaucer was here treating of any historical or personal situation whatsoever:

> Every detail of the poem is simply and adequately accounted for. The choice among the three suitors is a typical triple problem of love; the choice is left undecided in order to furnish a basis for animated social discussion, as is so often the case with the *demande d'amours;* the respite of a year is conditioned by the fact that the next assembly for choosing mates will occur on the next day of Saint Valentine.[2]

This poem, Professor Manly continues, is nothing more than 'a conventional love vision, in which the central situation is a *demande d'amours,* presented before a parliament of birds, presided over by a representative of the god or goddess of love, who in this case is Dame Nature.'[3]

Professor Farnham, facing this same question whether personal and historical allegory underlies the poem, or whether it is purely a piece of literary convention, answers somewhat more cautiously, with one foot in either camp.

> The *Parlement* beyond question holds a love problem, whether it has allegorical reference to a marriage in the royal house or not. The story presenting this love problem has certain features distinctive of *The Contending Lovers:*—arguments of the lovers based on love service and nobility, a court scene, a judge, general discussion, granting of choice to the maiden, an indefinite conclusion.

[2] J. M. Manly, *Festschrift für Lorenz Morsbach,* p. 287.
[3] *Ibid.,* p. 285.

These features are so unusual in combination that they settle the matter of a general relationship. The *Parlement* is a tale of contending lovers.[4]

This type of tale is found in very early literary productions, both in Oriental and Occidental sources. Giovanni da Prato's *Il Paradiso degli Alberti* was a popular example in the Middle Ages. Chaucer probably did not see Prato's work; but he did not need to, for the tale was current. Professor Farnham argues that in 'the light of *The Contending Lovers,* theories offering historical interpretation for the *Parlement* must inevitably be reconsidered.'[5] After remarking that 'A composite of the two theories is possible and offers an interpretation consistent with Chaucer's character,'[6] Professor Farnham concludes:

> What may and may not come to our knowledge in the future to throw further light on the *Parlement,* either in the way of more possible sources or in the way of more historical fact fortifying an allegorical interpretation, it is, of course, impossible to foretell.[7]

Professor Viktor Langhans in 1918 put forward a theory somewhat different from either; he considered the poem as a narrative exercise on the nature of love for St. Valentine's Day.[8]

Nevertheless, since the appearance of these studies, as before, scholars for the most part have continued to regard the *Parlement of Foules* as an allegory with a real personal and historical basis. Miss Edith Rickert

[4] W. E. Farnham, *P. M. L. A.*, XXXV, 321.

[5] *Ibid.*, XXXII, 518.

[6] *Ibid.*

[7] *Ibid.*

[8] V. Langhans, *Untersuchungen zu Chaucer,* 19ff.

in 1920, after surveying different theories as to the interpretation of the poem, summed up the case as follows:

> Without committing myself beyond the possibility of 'Retracciouns' to belief in the necessity of any historical interpretation, I feel at present that the peculiar features of the poem are not self-explanatory as belonging to either a triple *demande d'amours* or a mere exposition of natural as opposed to illicit love.[9]

Indeed, in the paper just mentioned, Miss Rickert herself proposes a new occasion for the composition of the poem:

> The plans of John of Gaunt for the marriage of his daughter Philippa seem from the evidence to have taken such shape in the late winter of 1381 as to make the production of such a poem as *The Parlement of Foules* a compliment which would have been particularly grateful to him, and the special development of the situation in the poem offered a plausible interpretation of the collapse of the most desirable plan, which the proud Duke could hardly have failed to appreciate.[10]

Nevertheless, one feels that the negotiations for the marriage of John of Gaunt's daughter fit very awkwardly with the situation presented in the poem, in which the formel is granted unreserved freedom of choice in selecting one of her pleading lovers. It does not appear that there was keen competition for the hand of Philippa of Lancaster, and our respect for Chaucer's tact must make us hesitate to believe that he wrote the *Parlement* 'as a court poet's balm for the hurt pride of the prince.'[11] Again, one may question

[9] As quoted in *Mod. Phil.*, XVIII, 29.

[10] *Ibid.*, p. 28.

[11] *Ibid.*, p. 26.

whether Chaucer, even to please his patron, would have risked the glaring inappropriateness of representing the young King as pleading for a woman many years his senior in the allegory of the wooing tercels and the demure formel.

Miss Rickert's theory, so far as I am aware, has not gained acceptance.[12] We are still free, therefore, to seek elsewhere for a clue to the meaning of the poem. And if we are to seek with any hope of success to connect the *Parlement of Foules* with the historical events of Chaucer's time, we must preface our task by surveying the historical background in an effort to trace the political movements and countermovements by which Chaucer was surrounded and in which he was involved.

[12] For a more extended study of Miss Rickert's theory see the review by M. E. Reid in *Univ. of Wisconsin Studies,* No. XVIII, pp. 60–70.

CHAPTER I

The Efforts in England to Establish Peace with France

THE Hundred Years' War had neither beginning nor end. The present brief survey confines itself to the period from the seventh decade almost down to the turn of the century, roughly from 1370 to 1398. The aim here is to review the series of diplomatic conventions which were held between England and France during this period in the effort to restore peace.

By 1370 the political situation had distinctly changed from what it was in the period of the Black Prince's victories at Crécy and Poitiers.[1] In 1367 after a temporary victory over the French in restoring the Castilian crown to Don Pedro the Black Prince returned to England. But he did not return flushed with success. He had been poorly paid for assisting the Castilian monarch, and besides he had contracted a sickness which practically incapacitated him and eventually resulted in his death. The very next year a French expedition replaced Enrico on the throne, and the military ascendency of the English abroad was thus summarily ended. This expedition was the last exploit performed

[1] In this historical study I have relied for the most part on the following authorities. *Les Grands Chroniques de France,* VI (ed. Paulin-Paris), 346ff. *Les Mémoires de Du Guesclin* (ed. Petitot), 156ff. E. Cosneau, *Les Grandes Traités de la Guerre de Cent Ans,* 69ff.

by the free companies of France. Charles V began thereafter the formation of a more formidable military corps. Realizing that his defeats at Crécy and Poitiers marked the end of chivalric modes of warfare, Charles V proceeded to establish a modern military system. His army was well equipped and well paid, and soon became a disciplined fighting machine. By 1373 an 'Ordonnance' signalled the advent of a complete military organization.[2]

Meanwhile, Edward III relied upon his commissioners to negotiate a satisfactory settlement with France. In his efforts to effect a satisfactory treaty with France, Edward was able to rely upon the assistance of Pope Gregory, whose energies were frequently employed in the difficult task of establishing peace.[3] In 1372, when Gregory was able to arrange a conference with the French, it appeared that a treaty might be negotiated. But Charles V, absorbed by ambitious war programs, was not then ready to conclude an agreement. In 1373, Edward, revived by false hopes, sought to renew the struggle, but 'avec plus d'energie, que de succés.' The Pope, however, continued to urge the two nations to treat for peace; and his legates accompanied the English envoys in their journey to France. At Bordeaux and again at Bruges, in 1374, representatives of the two nations met and the prospect of concluding a satisfactory treaty appeared bright. But the Duke of Lancaster, who represented the hopes of England, put forward extravagant demands. Ac-

[2] J. R. M. Macdonald, *A Hist. of France,* I, p. 256.

[3] G. Clement-Simon, *La Rupture du Traité de Bretigny,* 90ff. Cf. Barante, *Hist. des Ducs de Bourg.,* pp. 144–45.

cording to a contemporary chronicler,[4] the English 'requeroient a grant instance avoir les ressors et souverraintés des terres.' The French being undisposed to accede to these terms, the conference ended with a mere agreement to suspend hostilities for some two months. When the Duke of Lancaster returned to England, he was coldly welcomed by his father and eldest brother, who had expected a favorable treaty.[5]

The truce, in fact, did not last even two months. The victories of the persistent Du Guesclin and the perverse illness of the Black Prince placed Edward in an uncomfortable predicament and increased his anxiety. Yet nothing could be done except to arrange for another truce.

The friendly intervention of Gregory XI in 1375 was responsible for the series of truces and partial treaties which followed, one being concluded at Bourboug on February 11, 1375, and another more general treaty being later effected at Bruges. But shortly after, when the Count of Flanders entered the negotiations as a supporter of Charles V, the previous agreements were practically nullified, and Edward was faced with the difficulty of meeting the demands of both France and Flanders.[6]

The legates of the Holy See, whose efforts to effect a reconciliation between the two monarchs had been uniformly unsuccessful, attempted now to induce the powers of England, France, and Flanders to treat for peace. Edward accordingly dispatched the Duke of

[4] R. Delachenal, *Chronique des Régnes de Jean II et de Charles V*, II, pp. 176–77.

[5] G. Clement-Simon, *La Rupture du Traité de Brétigny*, 90–91.

[6] H. Moranville, *Chron. Reg. Franc.*, pp. 360ff. and notes.

Lancaster to Calais, to confer with Charles V's representatives. Lancaster, who had now been persuaded to a less ambitious policy, promised to aid in 'l'avancement du traité.' The envoys met at Bruges, the Duke of Bourgogne and the Bishop of Amiens representing the French, and the Duke of Lancaster, the Count of Salisbury, and the Bishop of London being sent by the English. A treaty was drawn up and signed by the envoys on June 27, 1375, which provided that peace should continue until May 1, 1376. An interesting contemporary document contains Edward's approval of this treaty.[7]

In the last two years of Edward's reign the prospects of peace brightened somewhat. According to the patriotic Christine de Pisan, Charles V, 'nonobstant sa bonne fortune en ses guerres et sa grant possance, se censenty à traictié de paix aux Angloiz.'[8] Toward the end of the year 1376, conferences held between the French and English prolonged the existing peace and proposed details to be ratified in a later treaty.

Exactly when the project of a marriage alliance with France was first broached it is impossible to say, but it was certainly under consideration in 1376. That Edward III should have interested himself in promoting a marriage alliance is not surprising, for such alliances were not infrequently employed by sovereigns in similar situations as a means of confirming treaties of peace.

The following statement by a contemporary chron-

[7] L. Gilliodts-Van Severen, *Le Cotton Manuscrit Galba B. I.*, 'Annexes, 3 F.,' p. 518ff. (*Acad. Roy. des Sciences de Belg.*, 1896.)

[8] From Christine de Pisan's *Livre des Fais et Bonnes Meurs du Sage Roy Charles V*, 40f.

icler in his account of the conferences of 1376 at 'Buenen'[9] and at Bruges establishes the fact that the ambassadors were not only discussing peace terms in general but were also considering a marriage between Marie, daughter of Charles V, and Richard, son of the Black Prince.

A° 1376. En cette année, les ambassadeurs du Saint Père et ceux des deux rois et de leurs alliés reprirent les conférences, tant à Buenen qu' à Bruges, pour traiter non seulement de la paix, mais encore du mariage de Marie, la fille aînée du roi Charles de France avec Richard, le neveu du prince Édouard de Galles.[10]

These meetings were of moment, for together with the English and French ambassadors were gathered the papal envoys ('de Saint Père') as well as Flemish and Norman representatives ('de leurs alliés'). About the meeting at Bruges, we gain further information from Froissart, who states that the King of England, 'après la fête Saint Michel,' formally invested young Richard as his successor; and 'en ce temps' dispatched several commissioners to Bruges, where they conferred with the French for a considerable time on the subject of the aforementioned marriage. Froissart's account is as follows.

Après la fête Saint Michel, que on eut fait à Londres l'obsèque du prince révéremment, le roi d'Angleterre fit reconnoître à ses enfants, le duc de Lancastre, le comte de Cantebruge (Cambridge), et monseigneur Thomas le mains-né (plus jeune), et tous les barons, comtes, prélats

[9] ? *Bouloigne,* the Latin form of which was *Bonona.*

[10] Gilliodts-Van Severen (*op. cit.,* p. 488) quotes this contemporary account. Richard was the Black Prince's son, and grandson to Edward III, but 'neveu,' the term employed by the chronicler, may in Old French also mean 'fils' or 'petit-fils.'

et chevaliers d'Angleterre, le jeune damoisel Richard à être roi après son décès; et leur fit aussi jurer solemnellement, et le fit seoir de-lez (près) lui le jour de Noël au dessus de tous ses enfants en état magestal, en remontrant et représentant qu'il seroit roi d'Angleterre après son décès. Si furent envoyés à Bruges en ce temps du côté des Anglois messire Jean sire de Gobeham (Cobham), l'évêque de Herford, le doyen de Londres; et de la partie des François, le comte de Salebruche (Saarbruck), le sire de Châtillon et maître Philebert l'Espoite. Et y étoient toudis (toujours) les prélats traiteurs qui toujours mettoient grand'peine que paix se fit; et traitèrent grand temps sur le mariage du jeune fils du prince et de madame Marie fille du roi de France. Et se partirent les parties tant de France que d'Angleterre et rapportèrent leur traités devers l'un roi et l'autre.[11]

The statements by the anonymous French chronicler and by Froissart are thus mutually corroborative. They receive further confirmation from the record in the *Exchequer Accounts* that Lord Cobham and his associates were sent to Bruges in 1376.[12]

Quite as interesting for our purpose as the date at which these marriage proposals were first discussed is the question whether the initiative in suggesting them was taken by France or by England. On this point Skeat remarks: 'Neither does it appear that discussion of the marriage arose on the English side; it was the French who proposed it, but the English who declined it, for the reason that they had received no instructions to that effect.' [13] But in this statement he is clearly mistaken. Fortunately, in determining the question we

[11] Buchon, *Les Chron. de J. Froissart,* VI, 101.

[12] Cf. Mirot and Déprez, 'Les Ambassades Anglaises,' *Bibl. de l'École des Chartes,* LX, Nos. CCCLXXVII–CCCLXXVIII, p. 196.

[13] Intro. *Minor Poems* (Oxford Chaucer, I), p. xxix.

have the benefit of an explicit statement by the King of France himself. In an official message sent 'aus gens de son Conseil' preparatory to the conference in 1377 he instructed his envoys as follows:

> *Item,* le roy ne veult pas que l'en parle de mariage de par lui, mais, se les Ainglois en faisoient mencion, l'en pourroit oir ce que diroient et après rapporter au roy.[14]

The French king's expectation that the English would bring up the subject was, of course, based upon his knowledge that it had been discussed at the earlier meetings of 1376. The attitude of Charles V in regard to the proposed alliance could hardly have been stated more explicitly. He does not wish to have it presented as his proposal, but if the English should bring the subject up his envoys are to hear what they have to say and then report to him.

In prosecuting the negotiations in 1377 for the marriage of Richard and Marie, Chaucer was personally concerned, making voyages to 'Montreuil,[15] Paris, and elsewhere.'[16] The story of Chaucer's part in this matrimonial conference, the lively hopes for its success, and its sudden termination following the death of Marie, must be studied in greater detail and are therefore reserved for special treatment in the following chapter.

Even after the failure of the negotiations of 1377 the English renewed their attempts to effect a marriage al-

[14] As quoted from official document by R. Delachenal in *Chron. des Régnes de Jean II et de Charles V,* III, 207.

[15] Montreuil-sur-mer, situated between Calais and Paris. This town passed into the possession of France in 1380.

[16] *Life Records,* No. 101. Emerson (*Rom. Rev.,* III, 355) slipped in stating that Chaucer saw in 1360 'the walls of Paris, probably for the only time in his life.'

liance with France. It appears from an official document that Chaucer was sent in the reign of Richard II to negotiate a marriage between 'the present King' and a French princess.[17] On the basis of this record, Skeat suggested that Chaucer was sent in January, 1378 with d'Angle, Hugh Segrave, and Walter Skirlawe.[18] But Chaucer is not mentioned with them in this deputation nor in their accounts to the Exchequer. It is quite as likely that he travelled in the company of Edward de Berkley, who followed d'Angle's group into Flanders shortly after January 26.[19] The fact that de Berkley and Chaucer were sent to Lombardy on May 28 would favor this supposition, for d'Angle and his associates did not return to England until May 30.[20]

In sending these royal commissioners to France to negotiate a marriage alliance in 1378 the English were

[17] *Life Records,* No. 143. The document itself bears date March 6, 1381, but the fact referred to was evidently somewhat earlier.

[18] Skeat, 'Intro.,' *Minor Poems,* xxxi.

[19] The royal deputation, dated January 16, is printed in Rymer, *Foedera,* Rec. Ed., IV, 28. See Skeat, *op. cit.,* xxxi. Excerpts from the *Exchequer Accounts* are printed in *Bibl. de l'École des Chartes,* LX, 198–99. Nos. CDIV and CDVI state that Walter Skirlawe and Guichard d'Angle were 'envoyé en *Flandre'* to treat of peace: Skirlawe from January 22 to May 31, d'Angle from January 26 to May 30. Edward de Berkley returned to England January 10, 1378, having been sent 'vers le roi de *Navarre* et en *Gascogne*.' Cf. *ibid.,* No. CCCLXXXIV, p. 197. His departure for Flanders followed that of the other commissioners aforementioned. Cf. Rymer, IV, 53.

[20] On Chaucer and Berkley see *Life Records,* p. 218. Their mission covered the dates May 28 to September 19. Cf. Berkley's account to the Exchequer in *Bibl. de l'École des Chartes,* LX, No. CDIX, p. 199. Cf. Kervyn de Lettenhove, *Œuvres de Froissart,* IX, 582, and notes.

entertaining false hopes; for the King of France was not inclined to listen to their proposals. Moreover, the English ambassadors did not arrive in Flanders until January 26, and all efforts to negotiate a marriage between King Richard and Princess Isabel would at once have been ended by the death of this princess on February 23, 1378. It appears, furthermore, that the Englishmen had expected to confer also with the Count of Flanders, but he declined to participate in the proposed conference.[21] The Duke of Bourgogne also sent his excuses. He was obliged to be in Paris, he explained, in order to assist in receiving his kinsman, the Emperor Charles IV, who was paying a visit to the French capital in the spring of 1378, on his tour of the Kingdom of France, so that he would be unable to attend the conference with the English ambassadors.[22] Finally, an agreement was out of the question as Charles V, having decided to turn his forces against the King of Navarre,[23] was now openly opposed to peace overtures from England.

This mission of 1378 has been the subject of a misunderstanding which it is necessary to clear up before

[21] Kervyn de Lettenhove (*Œuvres de Froissart,* IX, 582 in notes) prints a dispatch, dated May 3, 1378 (from the *Archives de Lille*), which reads: 'Les gens de II roys de France et d'Engleterre sont a Bruges, mais on tient de vray qu'il doyvent venir à Gand par devers monseigneur de Flandre avant qu'il se partichent.'

[22] Barante, *Hist. des Ducs de Bourgogne,* I, 70f. Cf. Anquetil, *Hist. de France,* V, 48.

[23] Secousse, *Hist. de Charles le Mauvais,* I, pt. II, 154f., 177. Cf. S. Luce, *Chron. des Quatre Premiers Valois,* 265f. Cf. Martene and Durand, *Thesaurus Anecdotum,* I, 1536ff.

we can interpret the facts correctly. Nicolas [24] thought this was the mission which Froissart reported under the date of 1377, and his statement of the case has recently been indorsed by Brusendorff.[25] But Nicolas failed to observe that the conferences of 1377 were held, as Froissart reported, at Montreuil and Calais, whereas the commissioners in 1378 were sent to Flanders. In the second place, the former negotiations were for the hand of Marie, whereas those of 1378 were for the hand of Isabel,[26] Charles V's sole surviving daughter. A third point which Nicolas overlooks is that two conferences were held in 1377,[27] whereas in 1378 the commissioners did not succeed in arranging a meeting with the French. Finally the chronicler names as the envoys who met the French at Calais: William de Montagu, Guischard d'Angle, and the Bishop of Herford, while the commissioners in 1378 consisted of an almost entirely different group. Guischard d'Angle was, of course, a commissioner in both years; though in the 1378 deputation he is referred to as Earl of Hunting-

[24] Nicolas, *Poetical Works of Chaucer,* I, 35–36. Froissart's account will be quoted in the following chapter.

[25] Brusendorff, *The Chaucer Tradition,* p. 161, n. 2.

[26] Ward (*Chaucer,* p. 77, in English Men of Letters) mistakenly names Marie as the princess who was the subject of these negotiations. Coulton (*Chaucer and His England,* 50f.) distinguishes the daughter as 'one of poor little Marie's sisters.' Marie died before 1378; Katherine was not born until February 4, 1378, and Isabel remained the only daughter to receive a proposal in January, 1378. Cf. Anselme, *Hist. généalogique,* I, 110d. Delisle, *Le Cab. des MSS. de la Bibl. Nat.,* III, 337ff. Delachenal, *Chron. des reg. de Jean II et de Charles V,* II, pp. 258, 272, 282, and notes.

[27] Cf. Nos. CCCXCV and CCCXCVII for the second conference. (*Bibl. de l'École des Chartes,* LX, p. 198.)

don, a title which he received at the beginning of Richard's reign. From this discussion it is clear that Nicolas was mistaken in interpreting Froissart's account as referring to the conference of 1378.

This historical survey has at least made it clear that England, as well as other European powers, repeatedly sought to gain alliance by marriage with France during the zenith of Charles V's reign.[28] Charles V was one of the richest kings in the Middle Ages.[29] The entertainment provided by the French King for the Emperor in 1378 was most elaborate and expensive. The Emperor's visit seems to have been one round of pleasure. He was invited to see the Louvre, to attend sumptuous banquets in his honor, to inspect the Hotel Saint-Paul, the palace Beaute-sur-Marne, and his *alma mater,* the University.[30] The King, Queen, and Dauphin gave the Emperor Charles costly gifts, and the Emperor responded by granting to the Dauphin the vicariate of the long extinct kingdom of Arles.[31] The court of France was at this time the mirror of fashion, the pink

[28] Secret letters touching a project of marriage between the King's son Louis and a daughter of Louis le Grand were exchanged by Charles and Louis. Cf. *Arch. Stor. per le prov. Nap.,* II, 107–57. It goes without saying that more than one country was interested in the Dauphin Charles. Italian ambassadors appear to have been in France in May, 1376–77, on a similar mission. Cf. Mas-Latrie, 'Nou. Preuves de l'Hist. de Chypre,' *Bibl. de l'École des Chartes,* XXXIV, 84.

[29] A. Lefévre, 'Apogée de Charles V (1377–78),' *Rev. de l'École d'Anthrop. de Paris,* XIII, 105f. Cf. A. Dieudonné, 'La Monnaie Royale de Charles V à Charles VI,' *Bibl. de l'École des Chartes,* LXXII, 473–79.

[30] Lefévre, *ibid.,* 117ff.

[31] J. R. M. Macdonald, *op. cit.,* 262.

of etiquette; and the king of France was regarded as an enemy to be feared and a powerful ally to be sought.

Before the Emperor returned home, however, sorrow came to the French royal family. Queen Jeanne died February 4, 1378, after giving birth to a daughter. This child was named Katherine.[32]

A paragraph may be devoted here to a brief sketch of the members of Charles V's family. The story of his daughters is not without interest in relation to the history we are studying. Charles V had married Jeanne de Bourbon in 1350, by whom he had nine children. The first four daughters hardly deserve mention in the present study. Three of them died in 1360 and a fourth, Jeanne, the mother's namesake, died in 1367. Although these four daughters are of little interest here, the case is reversed with the remaining three sisters, who are named Marie, Isabel, and Katherine. Marie and Isabel, as we have remarked, were the objects of marriage negotiations in 1377–78. In the chapter which follows an account of Marie will be given. Here it may be noted that their sister Katherine [33] was also made the object of England's marriage overtures after Isabel's death. It is to be observed, then, that all three of Charles V's daughters became at one time or another the subject of marriage proposals

[32] Cf. Christine de Pisan's account in *Livre des Fais et Bonnes Meurs du Sage Roy Charles V,* 100. Some discussion of Charles V's family will be found in *Biographie Universelle* and *La Grande Encyclopédie.* Cf. *Notes and Queries,* 3d Series, VII, 470.

[33] In 1386 Katherine married Jean de Berry, Count of Montpensier. She was the only daughter to survive Charles V who died in September, 1380. The King's sons, Lewis and the Dauphin Charles, likewise survived him.

from the royal family of England. If we are seeking the direction of England's political projects for marital alliances, all roads lead to France.

When Charles V offered to give his daughter Katherine to the English King (Richard II) in June, 1378, she was only an infant of five months of age. Whether or not the young age of the princess deterred the English, we do not know for certain. It would seem so; for though the French King was in 1378 prepared for the first time to make offers [34] on his own initiative, the English somewhat surprisingly refused this initial overture of the French. The next year, in 1379, a prince of Hungary sought Katherine's hand. Seeing a rival in the field, Richard II appeared in 1380 as a revived suitor; but as the French offered no other territory except lands in Aquitaine for the peace settlements, the opposing interests could not be reconciled. Everything in short conspired against the successful conclusion of this treaty for marriage.[35]

Although, as we have seen, negotiations with the French respecting treaties and marriage alliances continued as late as 1380, historians have recognized only one of the conferences after the settlements of the Treaty of Brétigny as productive of actual results. This was the conference of 1377, in which Chaucer figured and which we are to discuss in the following chapter.

It has been the purpose of the present chapter to

[34] Kervyn de Lettenhove (*Œuvres de Froissart,* XXIII, 350) has printed after MS. 2699 of Bibl. Nat. of Paris the 'mémoires des offres' which were made in Charles V's name by the Archbishops of Rouen and Ravenne at the Bouloigne conference of June, 1378.

[35] E. Lavisse, *Hist. de France,* IV, 246ff.

discuss Anglo-French relations; yet it would be giving the reader a false impression to allow him to believe that England did not maintain political relations with other countries as well. It does not appear that there were many plans for marriage alliances with other countries, however; and when the subject did come under discussion, it will be observed that foreign nations took the initiative in making marriage proposals. In 1379 Bernabo Visconti, Lord of Milan, directed to Richard II an overture in which the English King was to marry the Italian Lord's daughter Catarina. Chaucer paid a visit to Bernabo's court in 1378; and it has been suggested that he was sent as a matrimonial commissioner.[36] The record of his service on this mission indicates no more than that his purpose was military.[37] The advances which Bernabo made were, in any case, at length rejected.

England's political negotiations with the Emperor Charles IV and King Wenceslaus may be next considered. The facts in this case are soon stated. The Emperor Charles IV, shortly before his death (in

[36] Kirk (*Life Records,* xxviii) made this suggestion sometime ago. The following writers have also remarked on this possibility: Tatlock (*Dev. and Chron.,* 41–42), Cook (*Trans. Conn. Acad. Arts. and Sc.,* xx, 183), Kittredge (*Date of Ch's. Troilus,* 48), and Hulbert (*Ch's. Off. Life,* 48). For historical details see Rymer, *Rec. Ed.,* IV, 60; Walsingham, *Hist. Angl.* (Rolls Ed.), II, 46.

[37] Cf. *Life Records,* p. 218. In answer to an enquiry concerning Chaucer's Italian voyage and Catarina, Professor W. L. Bullock referred me to P. Litta's *Famiglie celebri l'Italia,* XIV, Iavola V. Mr. James A. Work has kindly consulted this volume for me in the Yale University Library. Litta informs us that Catarina married 'Giangaleazzo *Visconti* suo cugino' but fails to tell us more about Richard II.

1378), tried 'de faire mariage du dit roy d'Angleterre et de sa fille.' [38] Wenceslaus, King of the Romans, continued the Emperor's policy by proposing in 1379 and in 1380 a marriage between Richard II and his own sister Anne.[39] But the English seem to have been unattracted by these overtures; for from 1376 to 1380, as we have seen, English commissioners were actively engaged in efforts to establish a marital alliance and a peaceful relationship with their French neighbors. The political atmosphere of the time pointed clearly to France as the logical nation with which England wished to ally itself.

When the papal schism occurred, contemporary history was profoundly affected.[40] For one thing, papal dissension had the effect of severing Anglo-French relations. The later negotiations which led to the marriage of Richard II and Anne of Bohemia were directly instigated by the intervention of Pope Urban VI, who wished to keep England from associating itself with the supporters of his rival, Pope Clement VI. It was thus by an unexpected turn of events that an alliance with France was not effected. Fate in the form of the papal schism intervened.

History eventually rights its own story. There were many postponements before the French and English reached a final reconciliation. Postponed agreements were necessary; but the political outcome of the interests of these two countries was inevitable. A marriage alliance between the royal houses of England and France must some day be negotiated. In 1398 negotia-

[38] R. Delachenal, *Chron. des Rég. de Jean II et de Charles V*, II, 302f.

[39] Cf. Tatlock, *Dev. and Chron.*, 42.

[40] J. R. M. Macdonald, *A Hist. of France*, I, 263.

tions for the hand of a French princess were successful; and Richard II accordingly introduced Queen Isabella to the English court.[41]

[41] Sir Lewis Clifford, one of Chaucer's friends, figured in these negotiations. Cf. W. T. Waugh, 'The Lollard Knight,' *Scottish Historical Review,* XI, 61. Cf. Kittredge, *Mod. Phil.,* I, 1–18.

CHAPTER II

Chaucer's Part in the Marriage Negotiations of 1377

THERE are few more interesting years in Chaucer's life than the period of his service as marriage commissioner, although it is one which has received comparatively little attention. An investigation of the historical records dealing with this phase of Chaucer's activities has resulted in bringing to light in one or two cases new information in regard to these voyages abroad, and the persons with whom Chaucer was associated on these missions. Before taking up the record of Chaucer's part in the negotiations of 1377, we may inquire into his activities during the last quarter of the preceding year.

The conference of the English peace commissioners at Bruges, to which we referred in the preceding chapter, was held in November and December, 1376 'ad tractandum de pace inter ipsum dominum regem et adversarium suum Francie.' [1] From the accounts of the Exchequer we learn the names of these commissioners: William de Montague, Earl of Salisbury, sent on October 31 in company with John, King of Castille and Lyons (i.e., John of Gaunt), and Simon, Archbishop of Canterbury,[2] John de Cobeham, banneret, of

[1] *Exchequer Accounts* (unprinted), Q. R., E 101/317, No. 26.

[2] Cf. *Exchequer Accounts* (unprinted), Q. R., E 101/317, No. 23.

Kent, sent on the same date in company with the Bishop of Hereford 'et aliorum fidelium Regis,' [3] and Master John Schepeye, sent on November 2 'pro negociis regis.' [4] From Froissart we learn that at this conference not only terms of peace were considered but also proposals of the marriage of Richard and Marie were discussed.[5]

On December 23 Chaucer was sent abroad by the King in company with Sir John de Burley, Knight, on a confidential mission. Neither their destination nor the nature of their errand is disclosed in the Exchequer Roll, but there is good reason to surmise that they were employed in connection with these peace negotiations. The language employed in the commissions of Burley and Chaucer—'misso in secretis negociis Domini Regis' [6]—is very similar to that used with reference to the mission of Sir Thomas de Percy and Chaucer on February 17, 1377—'misso in nuncium in secretis negociis Domini Regis' [7]—and in the latter case, as we shall see presently, Chaucer at least was actually employed in the discussion of the peace treaties and marriage negotiations. Moreover, in 1378 Burley and Chaucer were again very probably associated in the mission to Lombardy which seems to have had among other objects the considerations of Duke Bernabo's proposal of a marriage between Richard II and his daughter Catarina.[8]

[3] See note 1.

[4] *Exchequer Accounts* (unprinted), Q. R., E 101/317, No. 24.

[5] Cf. Chapter I of the present study. See Kervyn de Lettenhove's *Froissart,* VIII, 382.

[6] Cf. *Life Records,* No. 98.

[7] *Ibid.,* No. 100.

[8] *Ibid.,* No. 122. But cf. Hulbert's remark on Burley in *Chaucer's Official Life,* 48.

Nicolas, finding no record of letters of protection issued to Burley and Chaucer, concluded that they were not actually sent abroad at this time.[9] On the other hand, as Kirk has pointed out,[10] Chaucer received a reward from the King on April 11, 1377, for 'divers voyages'[11] to foreign parts and this may easily allude not only to the mission from February to March, 1377, but also to this mission with Burley. Kirk's interpretation receives further support from a more recently published record,[12] dated May 10, 1377, in which Chaucer is mentioned as 'often abroad' on the King's service. Certainly, if Burley and Chaucer were sent in December, 1376 either to Flanders or France, it is more than likely that their errand related to the peace treaties and marriage proposals. It is to be noted that, according to the Exchequer Roll, they were sent 'per breue de priuato sigillo.' This is a form of commission which Déprez, an authority on mediæval diplomatic documents, states was often used by Edward III in the record of clerks sent to confer with messengers stationed elsewhere.[13]

When we come to February, 1377, Chaucer's personal participation in the negotiations for the marriage of Richard and Princess Marie is no longer a matter of inference but is established by positive evidence. On February 12, letters of protection, valid until Michaelmas, were issued to Geoffrey Chaucer, 'qui in

[9] Sir N. H. Nicolas, 'Memoir' in *Poetical Works of Chaucer,* I, 32.

[10] Cf. R. E. G. Kirk, *Life Records,* XXVI–VII.

[11] *Ibid.,* No. 103.

[12] Cf. *Cal. Pat. Rolls* (1374–1377), p. 462. Compare S. Moore's article in *Mod. Phil.,* XVI, 49f.

[13] See Eugéne Déprez's *Études de Diplomatique Anglaise,* 81.

obsequium Regis, in quibusdam secretis negociis Regis, ad partes transmarinas de precepto Regis profecturus est.' [14] In these letters his destination is mentioned in general terms, no doubt in order to cover any circumstances which might arise in the course of his mission, but from an entry in the Exchequer Roll five days later we learn that he was dispatched first to Flanders.

The Exchequer accounts of February 17 record a payment of £33 6s, 8d to Thomas de Percy, Knight and £10 to Chaucer. The mission on which they were sent is stated in identical terms: 'misso in nuncium in secretis negociis Domini Regis versus partes Flandric.' [15] It was obviously intended that the two envoys should travel together, but as to Sir Thomas de Percy's movements, or whether he actually departed on this mission, I can find no record. Froissart, in his account of the negotiations which followed, does not mention him, nor have I found record of the issuance of letters of protection to him, as was done in the case of Chaucer. I note that whereas the payment to Chaucer was 'per manus proprias' that to Sir Thomas de Percy was 'per manus Johannis Godard.' It is possible that a change was made at the last moment by substituting another person as Chaucer's fellow commissioner.

If this be the correct explanation, the person substituted for Sir Thomas de Percy was, in all probability, Sir Richard Stury, who was also sent abroad 'in obsequio Regis' on February 17 as appears from the following hitherto unpublished entry in the Exchequer Accounts of payments made to him for his expenses.

[14] *Life Records,* No. 99.
[15] *Ibid.,* No. 100.

Particule compoti Ricardi Stury militis de recepta misis & expensis suis in quodam viagio per ipsum facto eundo in obsequio Regis versus partes Francie anno LI°.

Idem onerat se de XXXIII li. VI s. VIII d. per ipsum receptis de Thesaurario & Camerariis ad Receptam scaccarii super vadiis & expensis eius eundo in viagio predicto per manus Walteri de Rothewelle clerici sui XIII die Februarii dicto anno LI°.

Summa recepte XXXIII li. VI s. VIII d.

Idem computat in vadiis suis in viagio predicto a XVII die Februarii dicto anno LI° quo die iter suum arripuit de Civitate Londonie versus partes predictas usque XXV (XXVII) diem Martii proxine sequentem quo die rediit ad regem apud Shene existentem videlicet per XXXVII dies utraque die computata ipso capiente per diem XXs. XXXVII (XXXIX) li. Et in passagio suo maris in viagio predicto XLVIs. XI d. Et in repassagio suo maris in eodem viagio LVI s. IIII d.

Summa expensarum: XLII li. IIIs. III d.

Et habet superplusagium VIII li. XVI s. VII d.[16]

It is significant that Stury and Chaucer not only went abroad on the same day but returned to England together on the same date.[17] Moreover, Froissart, in his account of the conference, mentions Stury's name along with Chaucer's as one of the English commissioners.

The commission to Chaucer, though it affords no information as to the purpose of the negotiations in which he was engaged, emphasizes the fact that they were highly confidential in their nature. This fact is important in distinguishing Chaucer's mission from that of the official ambassadors sent by Edward III

[16] *Exchequer Accounts,* Q. R., E 101/317, No. 32, hitherto unprinted.

[17] February 17 to March 25. According to *Enrolled Accts.* (F., 50 Edw. III, E.), Stury departed from London on February 13 and returned March 25.

on February 20 to treat with France on concluding a treaty of peace. The members of this formal deputation were the Bishop of Hereford, John de Cobeham, banneret, John de Montague, and Master John Shepeye.[18] We have a parallel case in 1389 in which official and confidential envoys were sent separately. In that year John and William Beauchamp, together with five others, were sent to Calais to treat for peace, and some days later Sir Richard Stury was sent thither by the Privy Council with separate instructions on what appears to have been a more confidential errand.[19]

Froissart in his account of the Anglo-French negotiations in the early months[20] of 1377 reports both the meetings of the official ambassadors and those of the confidential envoys. Moreover, from him we learn definitely the matters which were discussed by the group with which Chaucer was associated. This passage has been reprinted from Froissart in the *Life Records* (No. 102) and elsewhere, but it is so important for our purpose that the text must be quoted:

> Environ le quaremiel se fist une secres treti(é)s entre ces François et ces Englès, et deurent li Englès leurs trettiés porter en Engleterre, et li François en France, cascuns devers son signeur le roy, et devoient retourner, ou aultre commis que li roy renvoirent, à Moustruel sus mer; et sus cel estat furent les triewes ralongies jusque au premier

[18] Cf. Rymer, *Foedera,* III, pt. 11, 1073.

[19] Cf. Sir N. H. Nicolas, *Proceedings and Ordinances of the Privy Council,* I, 7f.

[20] Kervyn (*Œuvres de Froissart,* VIII, 383 and 473) erroneously followed M. Sandras in believing that Chaucer was first sent to France on April 17. Raynaud (*Chron. de J. Froissart,* VIII, 328) more correctly dates the conferences March, April, May. Chaucer's first mission to France (with Stury) occurred in February and March.

jour de may. Si en alèrent li Englès en Engleterre, et li François (revinrent) en France, et raporterent leurs trettiés, et recordèrent sus quel estat il estoient parti l'un de l'autre. Si furent envoiiet à Moustruel sus mer, dou costé des François, li sires de Couci, li sires de Riviere, messires Nicolas Brake et Nicolas le Mercier, et dou costé des Englès, messires Guichars d'angle, messires Richars Sturi et Joffrois Cauchies. Et parlementèrent cil signeur et ces parties grant temps sus le mariage dou jone Richard, fil dou prince, et de ma damoiselle Marie, fille dou Roy de France, et revinrent arrière en Engleterre, et raportèrent leurs trettiés, et ossi le François en France, et furent les triewes ralongies un mois.[21]

At this 'secret traité,' then, the subject discussed at length was that of the marriage of young prince Richard and Marie the daughter of the King of France. And the three English representatives at this conference were 'messires Guichars d'angles, messires Richars Sturi et Joffrois Cauchies [i.e., Chaucer].' Before proceeding to trace the results of their deliberations, it will be well to bring together the available information in regard to the two Englishmen who sat with Chaucer in this conference.

Sir Guischard d'Angle was a Frenchman by birth and training, who has left his record in the annals of the time as a valiant and chivalrous knight.[22] He fought

[21] S. Luce, *Chroniques de J. Froissart,* VIII, 225–26.

[22] See G. F. Beltz's biographical sketch in *Memorials of the Order of the Garter,* 182–87. There has been considerable confusion as to the form of his name. Skeat (*Minor Poems,* p. xxx) was misled by Stow (*Life Records,* No. 106) who mentions 'Sir Richard of Anglisisin, a Poyton'; but Stow followed an anonymous chronicler (cf. *Arch.,* XXII, 279, note O) who used the same spelling—'Sir Richard of Anglisisin.' Beltz (*op. cit.,* 182–87) gives his lineage correctly—'Guischard d'Angle,' eldest son of a father of the same name and of

with great courage at Poitiers in 1356, and was left for dead on the battle-field. He changed his allegiance from France to England, it is said, through his admiration for the romantic exploits of the Black Prince. Whether this be true or not, the latter appointed Sir Guischard Marshal of Aquitaine. He is later referred to as Lord of Playnmartyn and Captain of Aquitaine.[23] In 1369 he was sent to Rome by Edward III to confer with Urban V in regard to certain affairs pertaining to the said duchy of Aquitaine. While in Rome Sir Guischard met Froissart and shared his company on the homeward journey.[24] Sir Guischard was associated with the Black Prince until the latter's death, and when the Prince fell sick in 1376 he placed his young son Richard under the guardianship of this old warrior.[25]

Marguerite Maubert. The reader will observe that present-day writers err in calling him Richard; for he is not to be confused with a Frenchman 'Richard l'Ainglois,' whom Charles V (*Mandements et Actes Divers,* No. 114, p. 57) paid '100 florins d'or' for services in the year 1364. Walsingham (*Hist. Angl.,* I, 338) and other contemporary English chroniclers seem not to have known his correct name, for they call him 'd'Angoulême,' confusing his name with the French town of Angoulême; but he was born in Angle, a village in Clarenton in Poitou.

[23] Cf. *Cal. Pat. Rolls* (Feb. 1, 1366), p. 222. See entries of d'Angle's name in *John of Gaunt's Registrar,* ed. Armitage-Smith. Beltz (see preceding note) might have called attention to the fact that Sir Guischard had lost all favor with France by 1371 when King Charles V gave to Geoffrey de la Celle 'des terres confisquées sur Guischard d'Angle, partisan du roi d'Angleterre.' Cf. J. Delaville le Roulx, *La France en Orient au XIVe Siècle,* I, note 3 on pp. 190–91.

[24] Cf. G. L. Kittredge's valuable article 'Chaucer and Froissart,' *Engl. Stud.,* XXVI, 321–36.

[25] Cf. S. Luce's remarks in *Chron. de J. Froissart,* VIII, cxxxviii.

There was special propriety, therefore, in sending him to negotiate for the marriage of Richard and Marie. Furthermore, he had some experience in the capacity of marriage commissioner. It was he who first suggested to John of Gaunt a marriage with Constance of Castile. The conduct of these negotiations was entrusted to him in 1371, and under his management they were carried to success. As a soldier with the army of the Black Prince, he had served the cause of Constance's father, King Pedro, at the battle of Nagera in 1367. He was present at the famous interview between the Black Prince and Don Pedro and afterwards escorted Pedro to Burgos where the latter resumed his title to the Spanish throne. In 1372 Sir Guischard and other knights of Pembroke's troupe were taken prisoners by the supporters of Enrico, Pedro's brother, and they were held in captivity until they were released in 1374 as a result of negotiations between the English and Bertrand Du Guesclin and his cousin Oliver Mauny. It was more probably from Sir Guischard than from John of Gaunt that Chaucer learned the story of King Pedro of Spain which he includes in the *Monk's Tale*. On the death of Sir Guischard in 1380, the Duke of Lancaster ordered payments 'for 1000 masses sung for the soul of Guychard Dangle [26] and Thomas Banastre, dec'ed.'

Sir Richard Stury, the other English member in attendance at the secret conference, has received little attention from biographers. Nevertheless, he proves to be a person of wide influence who had very interesting connections. And Chaucer's personal relations with him were obviously closer than with Sir Guischard.

[26] Cf. Beltz, *op. cit.*, 186f.

Stury and Chaucer both served in the campaign of 1359–60 and both were taken prisoners by the French. £50 was paid for Stury's ransom and £16 for Chaucer's.[27] In 1368 the household accounts of Edward III show payments for robes for Christmas to Geoffrey and Philippa Chaucer, Lord Latimer, Robert de Assheton, and Richard Stury.[28] Their names appear together in a record dated July 26, 1377:[29] Chaucer as 'scutifer regis' and Stury as 'miles' receive payments for robes and the like. Many years later we find the poet and Stury again associated. In March, 1390, they were appointed members of a commission to repair the dikes and drains of the Thames from Greenwich to Woolwich.[30] It is interesting to note also that Stury, like Chaucer and Sir Guischard, was a personal friend of Froissart.[31] In July, 1394, while Stury was in attendance on Richard II at Eltham, Froissart again met his friend, and they walked in the vine-covered alleys of the palace as dusk came on.[32] A few days later, according to Froissart's account, it was Stury who introduced him to the King, when the chronicler presented His Majesty with the volume which he had brought all the way from France as a gift to him.[33] Sir Richard Stury, like Sir Guischard, had the advan-

[27] *Life Records,* No. 34.

[28] *Ibid.,* No. 53.

[29] *Ibid.,* No. 109.

[30] Cf. G. G. Coulton, *Chaucer and His England,* 62.

[31] F. S. Shears (*Froissart,* p. 19) refers to Stury as 'Froissart's great friend.' For this reference I am indebted to the kindness of Professor C. B. Millican.

[32] Cf. W. T. Waugh, 'The Lollard Knight,' *Scottish Hist. Rev.,* XI, 65.

[33] *Ibid.,* 69.

tage of diplomatic experience and had been entrusted with important political responsibilities. In 1370 he had been chosen to accompany Charles the Bad, King of Navarre, on his return to his own dominions.[34] In 1389 and 1390 he was sent to negotiate with France; and in 1394 he was member of a party including Lancaster and York which was empowered to treat for peace with the French. Returning from France, Stury was sent to the Border with the Earl of Northumberland and others to treat in regard to certain marriage alliances between the royal houses of England and Scotland.[35] During this same year (1394) he was appointed as one member of a group to receive the oath of the King of Scots.[36]

Stury was also a Knight of the Privy Chamber, and the frequent royal grants bestowed upon him testify to the high favor in which he was held by the King.[37] Finally, it may be noted that Sir Richard Stury, like Sir Lewis Clifford, was one of the Lollard Knights, and that both he and Sir Guischard d'Angle belonged to John of Gaunt's clique. Furthermore, it is important to remark that both Stury and d'Angle seem to have had literary interests and connections aside from their mutual friendship with Froissart and Chaucer. For example, Stury's possessions at his death included a manuscript of the *Roman de la Rose*.[38] In 1372 Sir Guischard was taken prisoner with Otto de Granson

[34] Stury's associate on this mission was Sir John Beauchamp. Cf. Hasted's *Kent* (Drake's ed.), pt. I, 215.

[35] Cf. J. Collinson, *Somerset,* I, 263.

[36] Cf. Hasted's *Kent,* pt. I, 215ff.

[37] *Ibid.* Cf. Waugh, *op. cit.,* 64f.

[38] *Cat. of MSS. Bibl. Reg.,* p. 297. Cf. Waugh, *op. cit.,* p. 70.

at Rochelle.[39] Granson is remembered in connection with Chaucer's *Compleynt of Venus,* a poem based on three of Sir Otto's 'balades.'[40]

The evidence already presented is sufficient to account for the sending of these persons as confidential envoys to discuss with the French the proposals of the marriage of Richard and Marie. But our understanding of the political situation would not be complete without recognizing the influence at court which seems to have controlled the movements of these commissioners.

The benefactress of Sir Richard Stury was none other than Alice Perrers, mistress of the aged King. It was Alice who joined with Richard Stury and Lord Latimer in securing the disgrace of Sir Peter de la Mare in 1376.[41] When the Good Parliament took action against Stury in this same year, he was restored to court favor through the intervention of Alice and John of Gaunt.[42] Sir Guischard d'Angle also, though long a partisan of the Black Prince, was later associated with the party of Alice Perrers and John of Gaunt. On August 20, 1376, only two months after the death of the Black Prince, we find Sir Guischard numbered in a group who helped to 'set free' Alice's husband, 'Williams de Wyndesore from the tower prison.'[43]

[39] Beltz, *op. cit.,* pp. 182–87. Cf. Buchon's *Froissart* (*Variantes*), VI, p. 78.

[40] Cf. A. Piaget, *Romania,* XIX, 237–39, 403–48.

[41] See the biographical sketch of Alice Perrers in *Dict. Nat. Biog.* Cf. *Chronicon Angliae* (ed. Maunde Thompson), 125f.

[42] Cf. Waugh, *op. cit.,* 65.

[43] Cf. *Cal. Close Rolls* (1374–1377), p. 443. The date of Alice's marriage to William de Wyndesore has been under discussion. 'Hermentrude' (*N. & Q.,* 7 S, VIII, 97f.) holds that

Every contemporary chronicler from Christine de Pisan to the pious Walsingham testifies that Alice held sway over Edward in his dotage. As Armitage-Smith puts it, Alice Perrers 'preserved her power over her dying lover. The fact was recognized by all, including William of Wykeham.' [44] Even the Pope, the head of Christendom, turned to her for assistance.[45] An anonymous chronicler, whose narrative is unusually rich in detail, adds the statement that Alice had under her control the conduct of the war:

> This woman, after she was in the Kyng's friendshipp, she so bewitched hym, that he permytted the warres & greatest matters of the realme to be defyned by her councell.[46]

The same chronicler also mentions Sir Richard Stury and Lord Latimer as Alice's political lieutenants.

> The foresayd Ales returneth to her vanitye, & she ys mayd so familier with the kynge with her companions, that yt ys to say the Lorde Latymer & Syr Ryrchard Stiry, that att there beck the kynge permitted all matters of the realme to be disposed, & commytted also to the government of hym selfe.[47]

It can hardly be doubted, then, that the appointment of Sir Guischard d'Angle, Sir Richard Stury, and Geoffrey Chaucer as confidential envoys was made with the con-

---

she was married while in Queen Philippa's service (as early as 1365). Although this date may or may not be correct, we need not hesitate to follow *Biographie Universelle* (in article 'Edouard III') in placing the date of her marriage before 1376.

[44] Armitage-Smith, *John of Gaunt,* 184.

[45] Cf. *Papal Letters,* IV, 96.

[46] Ed. T. Amyot, *Archæologia,* XXII, 233.

[47] *Ibid.,* 242. The editor of this chronicle believes it to have been written at the time of the incidents therein recounted.

sent, very possibly at the suggestion, of Alice Perrers. In this connection it is interesting to find the authoritative historian M. Siméon Luce, in his edition of Froissart, explaining in a footnote the mention of Chaucer as a member of this commission:

> Geoffroi Chaucer, le protégé de la favorite Alice Perrers et l'ami de Froissart, valet pensionnaire du roi d'Angleterre en 1367. . . .[48]

Our estimate of Chaucer's character need not be materially modified by this belated recognition of the political associations in which he was involved. If any one should be scandalized at the suggestion that Chaucer was a protégé of Alice Perrers, one should remember that she was also a staunch supporter of John Wyclif.

We are ready now to consider the results of this meeting at Montreuil-sur-mer of the English and French commissioners who 'parleyed for a long time over the marriage of the young Richard and Marie, the daughter of the French King.'[49] Froissart tells us that after drawing up a 'traité' the conference adjourned in order that the terms of the 'traité' might be reported to the sovereigns of the two nations. This certainly implies that the commissioners themselves had come to an agreement in regard to the proposals under discussion. Moreover, when the conference adjourned, it was arranged that the commissioners should reassemble on the first of May after the 'traité' had been referred for approval to their respective sovereigns. Unless the envoys had succeeded in coming to an agreement, they would hardly have fixed a date for resuming

[48] Cf. S. Luce, *Chron. de J. Froissart,* VIII, cxxxix, note 3.
[49] Cf. S. Luce, *Chron. de J. Froissart,* VIII, 225–26.

the negotiations. This is the view taken by the historians. Clement-Simon [50] remarks that the commissioners at this time had reason to anticipate that this marriage agreement would result in securing a permanent peace. And Simonde de Sismondi [51] declares that a treaty was negotiated which was to be bound by the marriage of young Richard and Marie.

Chaucer and Sir Richard Stury returned to England together, arriving on March 25, to present this gratifying report of the success of their negotiations. The Exchequer record of the payment to Stury, it should be observed, states that he returned 'ad regem apud Sheen.' In Chaucer's case the phrase used in the official document is 'de [a?] nostre dit ael' [52] (i.e., Edward III). Both forms of statement amount to the same thing. The aged king, steadily growing feebler, had retired to Sheen by March, 1377, where Alice Perrers remained by his bedside in constant attendance until his death on June 21. It was to Alice, undoubtedly, that Stury and Chaucer presented their report.

We may infer that the agreements drawn up by the confidential envoys at these conferences in February and March were favorably considered by Edward III and Charles V, inasmuch as commissioners were sent both by England and France to resume the negotiations

[50] Cf. *La Rupture du Traité de Bretigny,* 91–92. The historian says: 'La trêve est encore prorogée. Les legats restent sur la brèche, croient un moment pouvoir sceller la paix en mariant le fils du prince de Galles, héritier présomptif de la Couronne d'Angleterre, à Marie, fille du roi de France.'

[51] Cf. *Hist. des Français,* XI, 224f.

[52] Cf. *Life Records,* 'Additions,' No. 8. I had London photographers send me a photostat of this writ, the facsimile not being very clear. The word 'ael' is an Anglo-French spelling of 'aieul,' which in this case means 'grandfather.'

for peace on May 1, the date prearranged at the adjournment of the earlier conference.

Letters of protection were again issued to Chaucer on April 28, to be valid until August 1.[53] He must have gone abroad very shortly after this date, for from the appointment on May 10 of Thomas de Evesham [54] as the poet's deputy in administering the office of controller of customs and subsidies of wools, etc., it appears that Chaucer had already departed for France. Sir Richard Stury [55] seems not to have been sent on this second mission but to have remained in England. On the other hand, Sir Guischard d'Angle's name is included in the royal deputation [56] of April 28, and undoubtedly he met Chaucer in France on this second occasion. In fact, Froissart in his account of the renewed negotiations mentions Sir Guischard's name, but omits Chaucer's. Stow's account,[57] however, includes both Chaucer and Sir Guischard.

[53] *Life Records,* No. 104.

[54] *Cal. Pat. Rolls* (1374–1377), p. 462. Cf. S. Moore, *M. P.,* XVI, 49f.

[55] G. G. Coulton (*Chaucer and His England,* 51) mistakenly states that Chaucer was sent with Sir Guischard d'Angle and Sir Richard Stury to Montreuil in April, 1377.

[56] Rymer, *Foedera,* III, ii, 1076.

[57] Stow's account (cf. *Life Records,* No. 106) is based upon that of a contemporary chronicle which narrates the fate of the peace treaty from the English point of view. Cf. T. Amyot's edited reprint in *Archæologia,* XXII, 279, n. O. Neither Stow's report nor that of the contemporary chronicle is given an exact date. The *Life Records* incorrectly quote Stow's account under the date of April, for the meeting in France occurred in May. Moreover, the following hitherto unprinted writ of Williams de Montagu's mission makes it clear that the date of this commissioner's departure was actually May 1: 'Willelmus de Monte Acuto Comes Sarisbirie reddit compotum de cxxxiii li. vi. s. viii

The conference which met on May 1 to negotiate a peace treaty was more formal in its character than the meeting of the confidential envoys which took place in February and March. In the later conference the members of the royal deputation took the leading part. Also, in this case, instead of informal discussion between the English and French representatives the two parties met separately, the French at Montreuil and the English at Calais. Messengers were employed to transmit the proceedings of one party to the other.

But at all events the subject taken up for consideration at this conference was again the marriage of Prince Richard and Princess Marie of France. Froissart gives the following account of the conference and the failure of the negotiations to attain their object:

A ces parlemens et secrés trettiés qui furent assigné en le ville de Moustruel, furent envoiiet de par le roy de France li sires de Couci et messires Guillaumes des Dormans, canceliers de France: si s'en vinrent tenir à Moustruel. De le parties des Englès furent renvoiiet à Calais li contes de Sallebrin, [Salisbury] messires Guichars d'Angle, li evesques de Halfort [Hereford] et li evesques de Saint David, cancelier d'Engleterre. Et estoient là li trettieur qui aloient de l'un à l'autre, et qui portoient les trettiés, li archevesques de Ravane et li evesques de Carpentras. Et furent toudis leur parlement et leur trettié sus le mariage devant dit, et offroient li François, avocques leur dame, fille dou roy de France, douse cités ou royaume

---

d. de prefato sibi facto ad dictam receptriam primo die Maii anno LIo Regis Edwardi tertii super vadium ipsius Willelmi missi in Nuncium Regis Edwardi versus partes Calesie ad tractandum de pace inter ipsum Regum Edwardum & Adversarium suum Francie ibidem. Et. reddit in compoto suo inde alibi in hoc Reguo Regis computat(o). Et quietus est.' (From E/372/226, *Pipe Roll,* 4 Ric. II, Somerset and Dorset, hitherto unprinted.)

de France, c'est à entendre en la ducé d'Aquittaines, mais il voloient avoir Calais abatue. Si se desrompirent cil parlement et cil trettié, sans riens faire, car onques pour cose que cil trettieur seuissent dire, priier ne remoustrer, ces parties ne se veurent ou osèrent onques assegurer sus certainne place, entre la ville de Moustruel et Calais, pour yaus comparoir l'un devant l'autre. Si demorèrent les coses ensi, et ne furent les triewes plus ralongies, mais la guerre renouvelée, et retournèrent li François en France.[58]

Authorities differ in their statement of the causes which led to the breaking off of these treaties for peace. Simonde de Sismondi [59] may be right in believing that in the interval since the earlier meeting of the envoys the ambitions of Charles V had risen, so that he was disposed to obstruct the efforts of the plenipotentiaries. He knew, of course, that his once formidable rival, Edward III, was now virtually dying.

In any event there was a notable stiffening in the attitude of the ambassadors, and there was much haggling over some of the terms of the proposed treaty. The offer of twelve cities in the Duchy of Aquitaine as a dowry for the Princess Marie would hardly have appeared satisfactory to the English, inasmuch as this territory had only recently been conquered by Charles V and was therefore regarded by them as rightfully belonging to England. Nor were they disposed to acquiesce to the French demand that the defences of Calais be dismantled. Indeed, in the opinion of Longman,[60] it was this demand that caused the disruption of the negotiations. Froissart states that the existing truce expired and that, efforts to extend it being unsuccessful,

[58] S. Luce (and Raynaud), *Chron. de Froissart,* VIII, 227.
[59] *Hist. des Français,* XI, 224ff.
[60] *Edward III and His Times,* 271, note 1.

hostilities were resumed. But just when did the truce expire? Warburton states[61] that the existing truce ceased altogether before the death of Edward III, but he gives no evidence to support his statement. Du Guesclin,[62] on the other hand, declares: 'Au moment où Edouard mourut la trêve expiroit.' This would mean that the truce was in effect until June 21, and by implication that the peace negotiations continued almost until that date. Also, it is Beltz's opinion[63] that the negotiations for the marriage between Richard and Marie continued until they were frustrated by the death of the English King.

But in this matter not only the death of King Edward is to be considered, but also the death of the French princess. Before we can understand the actual situation, we must determine as precisely as possible the date of Princess Marie's death. Speaking of the decease of Edward III, Froissart adds: 'Assez tôt après tréspassa madame Marie.'[64] And subsequent historians have relied, apparently, on his authority. The only information as to Marie's death given by Anselme is, 'mourut jeune en 1377.'[65] It has been my good fortune to discover a piece of evidence, overlooked hitherto, which helps materially in fixing the time of Marie's death. The following item is included in a 'Mandement' of Charles V under date of May 30:

A Paris, 30 mai 1377

Charles—Nous sommes tenuz a Martine la Thierie, marchande de paris, en la somme de six vins et quatre

[61] *Edward III*, 232.

[62] *Les Mémoires de Du Guesclin*, 157.

[63] *Mem. of Order of Garter*, 182ff.

[64] Buchon, *Les Chron. de Froissart*, VI, 105f.

[65] Anselme, *Histoire généalogique*, I, 110D.

frans d'or . . . , c'est a savoir pour VI pieces et demie de cendaulz noirs larges, pour doubler le poille de nostre fille Marie, a VII frans la piece, valent XLII frans.[66]

The direction on this date for payment for material to be used for her 'poille' (mortuary drape) [67] fixes the date of Marie's death before May 30, almost a full month earlier than as stated by Froissart.

Moreover, since it is clear that negotiations for the marriage alliance would terminate abruptly on the death of the princess, we may ask whether this may not have been the immediate cause for the disruption of the negotiations.

Just when Chaucer returned to England is not certainly known. Although his letters of protection were valid until August 1, he received payment for only fourteen days' service 'between April 30 and June 26.' [68] This would seem to imply that his return was hastened by the death of the princess.

It is to be observed, in conclusion, that, so far as is now definitely known, Chaucer during his whole career served as a royal commissioner in only two marriage negotiations. We have seen (in the previous chapter) that the English embassy was unable to treat with the French ambassadors on this subject in January and February of 1378. It has been clearly demonstrated that the negotiations for the hand of the Princess Marie

[66] Cf. L. Delisle, *Mandements et Actes Divers de Charles V*, No. 1377 (Coll. de Doc. inédits, 1874), page 708. This reference to Marie is not recorded in the index of the volume.

[67] Professor Oliver Towles kindly directed me to another use of 'poille' in the sense of 'drap mortuaire.' Cf. *Miracles de Nostre Dame*, VIII (Soc. des Anc. Textes Français), page 192.

[68] Cf. Kirk, *Life Records*, pp. xxvi–vii.

in 1376 and 1377 marked the really crucial stage in this history of French and English diplomatic relationships, and that a peaceful settlement of the political relations between these two countries seems to have been promised by this marriage alliance, which was itself terminated by the Princess Marie's death in May, 1377.

CHAPTER III

The 'Parlement of Foules' in the Light of These Negotiations

THE circumstances of the actual negotiations for the marriage of Richard and Marie, in which Chaucer took an active part, show such significant points of resemblance to the situation presented in the *Parlement of Foules* that in all probability they would have been accepted long ago as furnishing the key to the allegory in this poem had it not been for certain chronological misconceptions which stood in the way of this interpretation.

Indeed, in 1877 Mr. F. G. Fleay, observing that Chaucer was appointed a commissioner to treat for the marriage of Richard and Marie, saw in this the theme of Chaucer's allegory:

> In the *Assembly of Fowls* (date 1378, as it refers to the embassy concerning the marriage of Richard II to the French king's daughter) we have the first of the Valentine's Day poems rightly grouped together by Mr. Furnivall.[1]

Unfortunately Fleay, apparently misled by the opinions

[1] Fleay, *Guide to Chaucer and Spenser,* p. 38. Furnivall, whom Fleay quotes, had written in 1871 in his *Trial-Forewords* (p. 22) as follows: '1378, Jan. 16. Chaucer perhaps goes with the Embassy to France, to negotiate a marriage with the French King's daughter Mary. The marriage, if arranged, is put off. The *Parlament of Foules* can hardly apply to this.' But Marie died in 1377.

of Nicolas,[2] believed that these negotiations took place in 1378, and consequently assigned Chaucer's poem to that year. For this he was sharply taken to task by Furnivall,[3] who was quick to detect the inconsistency between Fleay's interpretation of the poem and the assignment to the date 1378—the year following the death of Marie. But if he had investigated the historical documents, he would have perceived that the error in chronology was chargeable to Nicolas rather than to Fleay.

Furnivall's standing among Chaucerians was so high and his rejection of Fleay's view was so unqualified that from that time until the present no one has reconsidered the possibility of this interpretation of Chaucer's poem.

In the first chapter, however, I have called attention to the error into which Nicolas fell, and have shown that Froissart in his account was dealing with the negotiations in the early months of 1377. With this chronological difficulty cleared away we may turn once more to these historical events as supplying the most probable occasion for the *Parlement of Foules.*

Of the three 'tercel egles' who appear in the poem as suitors for the 'formel egle,' one—the 'royal tercel'—is kept so persistently in the foreground that he virtually monopolizes the reader's attention. He is the only one to whom the adjective 'royal' is applied; and the other tercels, as is expressly stated, are of lower 'degre.' So Dame Nature introduces the wooers in this manner:

[2] Nicolas's error in this matter has been discussed in Chapter I (see above, pp. 14–15).

[3] Cf. *Chaucer Society Essays,* p. 405, note 1.

> But natheles my ryghtful ordenaunce
> May I nat lete for al this world to wynne:
> That he that most is worthi shal begynne.
> The tercel egle, as that ye knowen wel,
> The foul ryal above you in degre (390–94).

When Dame Nature, at the formel's request, adjourned the *parlement* to a later session, she took the opportunity to state in plain terms which of the suitors was, in her opinion, the one to be accepted:

> But as for conscyl for to chese a make,
> If hit were resoun, certes thanne wolde I
> Conseyle yow the ryal tercel take,
> As seyde the tercelet ful skilfully,
> As for the gentilest and most worthy
> Which I have wroght so wel to my plesaunce
> That to yow oghte been a suffisaunce (631–37).

The choice of the formel, though postponed, is in the mind of the reader a foregone conclusion. Indeed, it is to be observed that Chaucer makes the formel betray the state of her feelings in a fashion which could not possibly be misunderstood either by the fourteenth or the twentieth-century reader. At the conclusion of the royal tercel's plea we read:

> Right so for shame al wexen gan the hewe
> Of this formel, whan she herde al this;
> She neyther answerde 'wel,' ne seyde amis,
> So sore abasshed was she (444–47).

The pleas of the other tercels produce no apparent impression, but after the speech of the royal tercel, the formel blushes furiously.

The preferential treatment of the royal tercel, on the other hand, is precisely what would be expected if this suitor represents the young prince Richard, whom the aged King on Christmas Day, 1376, publicly proclaimed as the successor to the Crown of England and whom John of Gaunt presented to the gathering at Westminster Palace.[4] Thus interpreted, Dame Nature's advice to the formel eagle becomes an expression of the ardent hopes of the poet, and of all Englishmen who looked forward to a marriage alliance which would end the war with France. And so obvious has this identification of the royal tercel appeared to Chaucerian scholars that it has been agreed to by every one who has regarded the poem as reflecting historical events.

We may next inquire in regard to the rivals of Richard for the hand of Marie. The second tercel in the *Parlement* urges that he has a superior claim on the ground of his longer service:

> I love hire bet than ye don, by Seynt Jon.
> Or, at the leste, I love as wel as ye,
> And lenger have served hire in my degre:
> And if she sholde have loved for long lovynge,
> To me alone hadde be the gerdonynge (451–55).

This again closely parallels the actual situation in the negotiations for the French princess, as one of Marie's suitors in 1377 had some years' standing as a wooer. On February 6, 1374, Charles V had deputed envoys to treat in his name regarding the marriage of his daughter Marie with William, son of Duke Albert of Bavaria.[5] Brantôme gives the following statement of the conditions imposed by the French King:

> Le roy Charles le Quint, traittant le mariage de madame Marie de France, sa fille, aveq Guillaume, conte de Haynaut, en l'an mil troys cens septante et quatre, stipula la

[4] Armitage-Smith, *John of Gaunt*, pp. 143–44.

[5] Devillers, *Cartulaire des Comtes de Hainaut*, VI, pt. I, 393.

renonciation du dit conte au droict du royaume et de Dauphine; ce que est ung grand poinct: et par la voyez-vous les contrarietez.[6]

On February 10, Albert charged five commissioners to outline a treaty of marriage.[7] This treaty was soon drawn up and submitted to Charles and Albert on March 3, 1374.[8] During this same year the French King gave his daughter Marie the present of a little crown, which seems to have been a token of the betrothal.[9] In any event, Charles V on March 16, 1375, sent letters 'confirmant le contrat de mariage de Marie, sa fille, avec Guillaume, fils aîné du duc Albert de Baviere.'[10] The existing betrothal would naturally be one of the points to come up for consideration in the conference of 1377. But that any objection on this score was soon overcome is to be inferred from the fact that both the French and English envoys agreed in their report favoring the marriage alliance of Richard and Marie. But William of Bavaria, like the second tercel, would clearly have had good reason for maintaining that this earlier contract gave him the superior claim. He continued to be an active suitor for Marie's hand in 1377, and had at that date served her some two years longer than his rival Richard.

Chaucer also introduces a third suitor for the formel eagle, though it will be noted that in the description of this third tercel there are few personal touches:

[6] *Œuvres Complètes de Brantôme* (ed. L. Lalanne), VIII, 53 and note.

[7] Devillers, *ibid.*

[8] *Ibid.*

[9] Cf. J. Labarte, *Inventaire du Mobilier de Charles V*, pp. 19ff. and notes.

[10] Devillers, *op. cit.*, 395.

I seye nat this by me, for I ne can
Don no servyse that may my lady plese;
But I dar seyn, I am hire trewest man
As to my dom, and faynest wolde hire please:
At shorte wordes, til that deth me sese
I wol ben hires, whether I wake or wynke,
And trewe in al that herte may bethynke (477–83).

Such knowledge as we have of the historical circumstances does not enable us to identify this third suitor. This does not necessarily mean that one did not exist. In view of the political importance of the French royal family in European affairs, it would require some hardihood to deny that there was a third person being considered for the hand of the young princess. And if there was another claimant, Chaucer as one of the commissioners would certainly have known about it. On the other hand, Chaucer may have thought it advisable to introduce a third suitor into his allegory even if he had no definite person in mind. For Farnham [11] has demonstrated that the poet was following the 'Contending Lovers' type, in which we have a formula situation of three suitors and a maiden. Literary convention would, therefore, have strongly influenced the introduction of three suitors. Moreover, if he invented a third suitor in order to make his allegory conform to the general scheme of the 'Contending Lovers' tale, Chaucer would at the same time have subtly stressed the rivalry for the hand of the French princess. A contest in which William was presented as Richard's sole competitor would not have been overflattering to either the French or English court.

One of the points in Chaucer's allegory which has not hitherto been satisfactorily explained is the adjourn-

[11] *P. M. L. A.*, XXXII, 492–518.

ment of the *parlement* without an announcement of the formel eagle's choice. Since in this respect Chaucer departs notably from the conventional situation in the story of the 'Contending Lovers,' it is likely that he had a definite reason for this variation. What could have been Chaucer's reason for introducing this variation? Professor Manly, who interprets the poem as a conventional *demande d'amours,* declares that 'the choice is left undecided in order to furnish a basis for animated social discussion.'[12] But if Chaucer had been playing for a 'Lady or the Tiger' ending, he was guilty of a serious artistic lapse in showing such obvious partiality toward the royal tercel. And, as we have already remarked, when he allowed the formel to betray herself by blushing at the tercel eagle's declaration, he gave his case away completely. However animated may have been the social discussion provoked by the allegory, it certainly would not have been protracted. Professor Emerson,[13] on the other hand, would explain the inconclusive ending as due to Chaucer's desire to impress the reader with the formel's bashful coyness. But after her forthright declaration—

> I wol noght serven Venus ne Cupyde
> For sothe as yet, by no manere wey (652–53)—

was this really necessary? Under the continued persuasions of Dame Nature, the formel might have been permitted to stammer out a reluctant decision without any sacrifice of maidenly reserve. But if Chaucer was alluding to the negotiations for the princess Marie, the adjournment of the *parlement* strictly conformed to his-

[12] Manly, *Festschrift für Morsbach,* p. 287.
[13] *Jour. of Eng. and Germ. Phil.,* XIII, 573f.

torical fact. The commissioners in their discussions of February and March, though they had reached an agreement among themselves, adjourned until May 1 in order to report their treaties to their respective sovereigns. And Chaucer, no matter how hopeful he may have been of the ultimate success of the negotiations, was too good a diplomat to represent the project as a *fait accompli.* The situation presented in the poem, therefore, agrees exactly with the status of the marriage negotiations as it must have appeared to Chaucer when he returned to England on March 25, 1377.

Chaucer represents the birds as assembling 'on seynt Valentynes day,' and this was an anniversary which suited better than any other the theme of his poem.[14] Thereby also the *Parlement of Foules* was formally put forth as a Valentine Day poem—a type of which there were numerous representatives in the fourteenth century.[15] But though convention may have been a sufficient reason for the choice of this date for the assembly of the birds, it is interesting to observe that the date on which Chaucer and Stury set out from England on their confidential mission was February 17.

More significant, because free from the complication of literary convention, is the astronomical allusion which Chaucer introduces into the text of his poem:

> As wisly as I saw thee [Venus] north-north-west,
> When I began my sweven for to wryte (117–18).[16]

[14] Froissart dates the conference 'Environ le quareme.' In 1377 the first day in Lent was February 11, and Buchon dates the chronicler's account as the middle of February.

[15] Manly (*Festschrift für Morsbach,* 286f.) discusses this type of poem, and also refers to Piaget's study in *Romania,* XIX, 406ff.

[16] It will be noted that Chaucer used the preterit form. This

Chaucerian scholars are agreed in regarding the poet's allusions to astronomical phenomena as offering valuable testimony in chronological matters. The *Treatise on the Astrolabe* is sufficient evidence of his interest in astrological calculations. And within the last few years Professor Root [17] discovered an astronomical allusion in *Troilus and Cressida* which supplies most important evidence for dating that poem. There is good reason, therefore, to suppose that Chaucer's reference to the position of Venus was based upon actual observation.

Commentators have repeatedly discussed this line in the *Parlement of Foules* and have endeavored to find in it evidence which would help to date the poem. But their conclusions are not altogether consistent. Skeat [18] rightly regarded Chaucer's allusion as a reference to the planet Venus, which, since it is never more than 47° from the sun, must have been visible to the north of the west point at sunset. Skeat thereupon inferred that the poem was written in the spring or summer. Koch [19] shifts repeatedly in his date for the poem: in 1877 he favored the date 1381; in 1880 he preferred 1380, emending 'north north west' to 'west north west'; in 1903 he returned to the date 1381; and finally in 1921 he fixed upon April, 1382, as the date. Professor Manly [20] criticises Koch's dates and affirms that

suggests that the astronomical allusion may have been added as a postscript for the purpose of dating his poem. Otherwise he would have hardly said at an early point in the poem, 'When I began.'

[17] *P. M. L. A.*, XXXIX, pp. 49–63.

[18] Notes to *P. F. in Minor Poems* (Oxford, I), p. 509.

[19] Brusendorff (*The Chaucer Tradition*, p. 389, note 3) calls attention to Koch's dating.

[20] *Festschrift für Morsbach*, 289ff.

Venus would have been in the position described by Chaucer in the years 1374, 1375, 1377, 1379, 1380, 1382, and 1383.

I have referred the question to Professor Harlow Shapley of Harvard University and Professor P. H. Graham of New York University, and the statements which follow are based upon their replies.[21] While terrestrial observers might have seen Venus in the position stated on each of the years given by Professor Manly, the only years between 1372 and 1384 in which Venus would have been visible as an evening star *to an observer in the latitude of England* were 1374, 1377, and 1382. Of these three dates, 1374 is manifestly too early to be considered for the *Parlement* and in 1382 Richard II was already married and could hardly have figured as a bird suitor. We are left therefore with 1377 as the only available year. The extreme limits of the period of Venus's visibility as evening star in 1377 were February 15 to September 5. Venus would have been in the correct position to be an evening star as early as March, though much fainter than when ordinarily given this name. Moreover, at this time it was not far enough north to be in the north north west,[22] even if the observer were in England. The conditions for the phenomenon as Chaucer depicted it were fulfilled in April and May. In August, 1377, the planet attained its greatest brilliancy; but after July 1 it

[21] I wish to acknowledge a similar indebtedness to Miss Jennie Mohr of Harvard College Observatory for certain astronomical computations. The mathematician may consult 'Astronomical Papers,' vi, pt. III (Washington, 1895), pp. 271–382.

[22] Venus is never strictly NNW. Chaucer's phrase equals 'northwest,' and the first *north* is to be recognized as a poetic intensive.

would be so near the equator that by no stretch of the imagination could it be considered in the northwest, except for an observer in very high latitudes—Iceland, for instance. From these astronomical data we conclude, then, that if Chaucer wrote the *Parlement* in April, 1377, his allusion to Venus as north-north-west would have tallied with its actual position in the sky.

With this indication that the *Parlement* was composed in the interval between the two sessions of the commission treating for a marriage alliance, it is possible to perceive a double meaning in the somewhat enigmatical stanza with which the poem concludes. The noise made by the birds at their departing, Chaucer says, awakened him, and he betook him to his books—

> To rede upon, and yet I rede alway;
> I hope, ywis, to rede so som day
> That I shal mete som thing for to fare
> The bet; and thus to rede I wil not spare.

In these lines, scholars have suspected with good reason, the poet was hinting at the reward which he hoped might follow. Even so, it is hardly possible that Chaucer meant to say merely: 'I keep on reading my books in the hope that some day I shall read so that it will cause me to dream something to my profit; therefore I shall not give up my reading.' However, the verb 'reden,' which is repeated four times in these four lines, has as its primary significance to counsel or advise. Indeed, in this very poem (lines 566 and 579) it is used in this sense. It may be therefore that in this passage Chaucer is playing on the double meaning [23] of the word:

[23] A similar word-play is to be noted in the case of 'mete' (line 698), which Chaucer uses in a two-fold sense: (1) to dream, and (2) to meet with.—C. B.

(1) to 'read' in the modern sense, (2) to counsel or advise, alluding to his service as an envoy to treat for the marriage alliance. Thus interpreted, Chaucer's lines would convey a delicate assurance that he would continue to devote himself to the accomplishment of the diplomatic errand which had been entrusted to him. This interpretation would at least save the passage from what would otherwise be incredible banality. And if, as some scholars have suggested, the lines *were* intended as a hint on the part of the poet, we may see some significance in the fact that Chaucer actually received on April 11, 1377, a royal grant of £20.

In concluding, it would seem worthy of remark that scholars have felt it strange that Chaucer, after his account of the formel and her suitors, should have left it incomplete and never have returned to it again. Some have even attempted to find in other poems far-fetched references to the marriage which the reader fully expects will follow. However, whatever plans Chaucer may have cherished for a sequel to the *Parlement,* he never carried them into execution. And we may believe that the sudden death of the Princess Marie in May was the real reason why the story of the suspended *Parlement* was never followed by an epithalamium.

CHAPTER IV

The Koch-Emerson Theory

THE interpretation of the allegory in the *Parlement of Foules* which still receives widest acceptance today and also the date assigned to this poem by Chaucerian chronologists were first proposed by Professor John Koch in 1877.[1]

Though other scholars before him had regarded the *Parlement* as written to celebrate a royal courtship, Koch was the first to propose the year 1381 as the definite date for its composition. In support of this date, he presented two arguments. In the first, he maintained that the *Parlement of Foules* must have been written *later* than *Troilus and Cressida,* since it 'manifests an author of far greater skill than that of the latter work.'[2] 'Is it likely,' he asks, 'that Chaucer, after having overcome the contrast between realism and sentimentality in the *Parlement of Foules,* should have again fallen back into a vain struggle between the two in his next production? This would contradict all experience of development of character.'[3]

The second argument, which he presented as a corollary to the first, put forward as the motivating theme of the *Parlement* the negotiations for the marriage of Richard and Anne of Bohemia in the year 1381:

[1] *Englische Studien,* I, 287ff.; trans. in *Essays on Chaucer* (Chaucer Soc. Publ.), IV, 400ff.

[2] *Essays on Chaucer,* p. 405.

[3] *Ibid.,* pp. 405–06.

So I have reached—and methinks quite naturally—the year 1381 as the date of the *Parlament*. And in this year King Richard of England sent his ambassadors to Germany to woo Anne of Bohemia for him.[4]

The æsthetic argument advanced by Professor Koch for the date of the *Parlement* can be regarded today only as a curiosity in Chaucerian criticism. But his attempt to connect the poem with Richard and Anne won immediate acceptance, and is still endorsed by many Chaucer scholars. The evidence for this theory must, therefore, be carefully examined.

We may first consider Professor Koch's identification of the two tercels who appear in the *Parlement* as the rival suitors of Richard II. For these Koch selected two earlier suitors of Anne, William of Bavaria and Frederick of Meissen. The former of these, it is true, had been affianced to Anne at one time, but by 1373 the match had been definitely broken off. Moreover, as we have shown in the preceding chapter, William of Bavaria in 1374 was engaged to Princess Marie and their betrothal still continued in 1377. Nor did he figure at any later time as a suitor of Anne. Chaucer surely would have been too tactful to revive this earlier engagement, which ended unfortunately, in a poem written to celebrate the betrothal of Richard and Anne.

The impossibility of Koch's identification of William as the second tercel was clearly perceived and forcefully stated by Professor O. F. Emerson:

It must have occurred to others than Professor Koch that it was a strange procedure on Chaucer's part to introduce, as a rival suitor for Richard, one whose betrothal had

[4] *Ibid.*, p. 406.

been broken off as early as 1373, at least seven, perhaps nine years, before the time of the poem. Others may have wondered what reason we have to suppose that Chaucer even knew of such an engagement. Such news would surely not have had international circulation, nor would it have been freely communicated to those interested in this new match. At any rate Chaucer would scarcely have been likely to use this long past betrothal, if there had been a more active suitor in the field. As such a suitor may now be presented with confidence, we may safely dismiss William of Baiern-Holland.[5]

Professor Samuel Moore has added still other reasons for ruling out the Bavarian prince, and I may quote from the summary with which he concludes his discussion:

> These facts make it evident that Chaucer in 1380 or 1381 could not have intended to represent Guillaume de Baviere as a suitor for the hand of Anne. If we had still any doubt upon the point, that doubt would be resolved by the fact that on her journey from Bohemia to England at the end of the year 1381, to be married to Richard, Anne was for three or four days the guest of Albert and his duchess at Ath. We would have no better evidence of the friendly feeling that existed between the families of Guillaume and Anne.[6]

Accordingly it became necessary to propose another suitor for the hand of Anne to replace the disqualified William, and for this purpose Professor Emerson brought forward the dauphin of France, afterwards Charles VI. It is in this emended form that the Richard-Anne interpretation has continued to be a subject of discussion among Chaucerian scholars.

It soon appeared, however, that Professor Emerson

[5] *Mod. Phil.*, VIII, 47.

[6] *Mod. Lang. Notes*, XXVI, 10–11.

was as unfortunate with his candidate as Koch had been with William of Bavaria. Miss Rickert shows conclusively that the dauphin was never Anne's suitor. Valois, to whom Emerson had appealed, expressly referred to the hopes for an alliance with the dauphin Charles as *'a last illusion, entertained at this time by some Clementists.'* [7] Miss Rickert shows further that Froissart in mentioning the dying injunction of Charles V: 'Seek in Germany for the marriage of Charles my son,' [8] interpreted it as referring to the alliance with Isabel of Bavaria, instead of to a marriage with Anne, as Professor Emerson had argued.[9]

The remaining suitor, both Koch and Emerson would identify as Frederick of Meissen. But the selection of Frederick was also singularly unfortunate. Frederick, it is true, had been betrothed to Anne in 1373, but their betrothal was terminated about 1377 by Anne's family for political reasons.[10] How, then, could he figure five years later among Anne's suitors, unless, indeed, Chaucer was intending this as a list of trophies? Neither Anne, nor still less Richard we may be sure, would have been complimented by the introduction into the

[7] Quotation and italics as in Miss Rickert's study, *Mod. Phil.*, XVIII, 7. Emerson (*Mod. Phil.*, VIII, 52ff.) began his quotation from Valois one sentence after this rather significant statement.

[8] As quoted by Miss Rickert in *Mod. Phil.*, XVIII, 8f. The historical student might wish to recall that the Emperor did appear *interested* in an alliance with France in 1378, when he exchanged private letters (unknown to contemporaries) with Charles V relating to the marriage of the French king's son Lewis and Catherine of Hungary. Cf. N. Valois, *Ann. Bull. de la Soc. de l'Hist. de France* (year 1893), pp. 209–23.

[9] *Mod. Phil.*, VIII, 51ff. T. W. Douglas (*M. L. N.*, XLIII, 378–84) accepts Miss Rickert's historical evidence.

[10] Rickert, *op. cit.*, 6f.

competition of a candidate discarded years before. And, then, to represent her as hesitating in her choice would have been nothing less than a deliberate insult. We see, therefore, that neither Koch nor Emerson has been able to present a single suitor who has the necessary qualifications to be Richard's rival. But, in connecting the *Parlement* with the negotiations in which Richard and William figured as suitors for the hand of princess Marie, the allegory is interpreted on the basis of the actual situation existing in 1377.

Accordingly, if any one should be disposed to object to the Richard-Marie interpretation on the ground that I have succeeded in identifying only one of Richard's rivals, it will be seen that even in this respect Koch's and Emerson's interpretations are less satisfactory. Moreover, according to the interpretation here proposed it is not necessary to drag in persons or incidents from an earlier period.

The objections to the Richard-Anne interpretation raised by Professor Manly are fundamental, inasmuch as they strike at the very basis of that theory. The *Parlement,* he argues, if intended for presentation to Richard and Anne, would necessarily have been regarded by both as uncomplimentary:

> Can we suppose that either would be satisfied to have the situation left as it is? Years after her marriage a lady may be flattered by an allusion to the difficulty she had in choosing among her suitors, but at or near the time of the wedding to represent her as unable to decide is not a compliment but a joke, and a joke not in the best taste.
>
> If the poem was written before Anne's arrival in England, in Dec. 1381, it is difficult to see how it can have been intended for her. She could not have known of it unless Chaucer had sent it to her in Bohemia, and this,

while possible, is highly improbable. It must, therefore, if written at this time, have been intended as a compliment to Richard. But can anyone seriously maintain that Richard would have regarded it as complimentary, or that Chaucer, a courtier and an artist, could have supposed that it would be acceptable to him? It is true that, according to the current theory, Richard is represented by the first of the suitors; but the lady is represented as unable to decide whether to choose him, or an insignificant princeling, or that rival whom he called, not king of France, but 'nostre adversaire.'[11]

The cogency of Manly's arguments would no doubt have won universal acceptance had it not been for the instinctive feeling of many persons that Chaucer wrote this poem with a definite occasion in mind. And Manly had no other historical situation to propose as a substitute. Professor Emerson's attempt to parry Manly's objections can hardly be said to meet the point:

That Chaucer might have made it [i.e., the poem] more flattering to either or both is doubtless true. Why he did not do this we shall perhaps never know.[12]
Surely this [i.e., the indecision] did not indicate that Anne was 'unable to decide,' but rather that she thought it unmaidenly and unconventional to make her choice so quickly.[13]

Whatever might have been demanded by a delicate sense of maidenly propriety, the historical facts show that Anne not only did not hesitate in her choice but that she actually took an active part in promoting the marriage negotiations. The first suggestion of a marriage between Richard and Anne was made by her

[11] *Festschrift für Lorenz Morsbach,* 279–80.

[12] *Jour. of Eng. and Germ. Phil.,* XIII, 570.

[13] *Ibid.,* 573–74. Miss Rickert (*op. cit.,* 5–15) has further discussed Emerson's reply.

father the Emperor Charles IV, who treated for her betrothal to Richard II in 1378, but without success.[14] After the death of the Emperor later in the same year, Anne herself joined with her mother in renewing proposals for her marriage to Richard.[15] In 1379 her brother Wenceslas, King of the Romans, very possibly with the marriage alliance in view, opened correspondence with Richard II in the endeavor to persuade him to recognize Urban VI as the legitimate pope. In any case, when England decided for Pope Urban the result was immediately to expedite the marriage negotiations. On December 20, 1380, Richard announced that he had chosen Anne as his queen, and at Epiphany, 1381, plenipotentiaries from both kingdoms met in Flanders to arrange the conditions. January 23, 1381, Anne in her own person appointed ambassadors to treat; and early in May it was agreed that she should be received by the English envoys on the following Michaelmas. She landed at Dover about December 18, 1381, and was welcomed by the people with enthusiasm as the future queen of England. Following this series of diplomatic conferences and public ceremonies, the marriage was actually solemnized January 14, 1382.[16]

Contrast these facts, now, with the situation presented in the *Parlement*. The 'formel egle' remains passive throughout and even repels the friendly advice offered by Dame Nature that she accept the royal tercel.

[14] Delachenal, *Chron. des Reg. de Jean II et de Charles V*, III, p. 302. I do not know that this reference has been quoted by Koch-Emerson theorists.

[15] Cf. Rickert, *Mod. Phil.*, XVIII, p. 5, n. 1.

[16] I here follow Tatlock, *Development and Chron. of Chaucer*, p. 42.

> Almighty quene, unto this yeer be doon
> I aske respit for to avysen me;
> And after that to have my choys al free.
> This al and som that I wolde speke and seye;
> Ye gete no more, although ye do me deye.
> I wol noght serven Venus ne Cupyde
> For sothe as yet, by no manere way (647–53).

These are the formel's final words, and Dame Nature is obliged to make the best of the situation and adjourn the 'parlement' with comforting words to the rival suitors. It is unnecessary to emphasize the contradiction between the behavior of the 'formel egle' and the historical facts.

Professor Lange admits the distortion of history in the *Parlement* but explains it as a deliberate attempt on Chaucer's part to make the poem less uncomplimentary to Anne:

> Um den historischen tatsachen gegenüber vollig freie hand zu haben, sucht der dichter die form der allegorie. Wenn in *P. F.* die wahl rein auf seiten des adlerweibchens ist, so war das in wirklichkeit ganz anders. Wie entwurdigend wäre es für Anna, die tochter eines Kaisers, gewesen, hätte sie sich in der dichtung sofort entschlossen, den antrag des Königs von England anzunehmen.[17]

But while this reversal of the facts might have saved Anne's face, would it have been relished by Richard or by the English people for whom the poem was written? Moreover, it must be remembered that Richard had publicly announced his selection of Anne as his queen more than a year before the marriage took place. Professor Manly is fully justified in objecting:

> Would a poet of intelligence and tact represent her at this time as undecided in her choice, whereas her very

[17] H. Lange, *Anglia,* XL, 395.

presence in England was due to her having decided in favor of Richard? Surely, if Chaucer had planned to write a poem complimentary to both, it would have been easy to continue and complete this poem in such a way as to make it a clear and unequivocal compliment.[18]

This inconclusive ending of the *Parlement* is perhaps the most decisive objection to the Richard-Anne theory. The adherents of this theory agree in assigning the composition of the poem to the year 1382,[19] and the allusion to Venus as 'north-north-west' makes impossible an earlier date than March 24, since Venus's period as an evening star in 1382 began on that day.[20] This obliges us to suppose that Chaucer waited more than two months after the royal wedding before sitting down to write his allegory dealing with the competition among the suitors for Anne's hand, and that even then he concluded his poem without a definite mention of the marriage or even the betrothal. It is not strange that this situation should have perplexed even such a stout defender of the Richard-Anne theory as Professor Emerson:

It seems impossible that the poem could have been written in the latter year 1382 without some more definite reference to the marriage, or at least the accomplished betrothal of Richard and Anne.[21]

[18] *Festschrift für Morsbach,* 279–80.

[19] Lange, *Anglia,* XL, 395. Pollard, *Chaucer Primer,* pp. 50, 90. Koch, *Chronology,* p. 38.

[20] Professor Koch, indeed, in his latest statement dates the *Parlement* 'April, 1382.' *Englische Studien,* LV, 224f.

Other years have been suggested, but as I have shown in Chapter III, Venus was not visible in the correct latitude in the period 1378–1381.

[21] *Mod. Lang. Notes,* XXVI, 110–11.

None of these difficulties is encountered, however, if the poem is referred to the marriage negotiations of Richard and Marie. In this case, the marriage overtures did come from the English side, and not the other way round, as in the case of Anne. The inconclusive ending is explained as an allusion to the deferring of formal acceptance at the first conference in March, 1377. Moreover, with this as the occasion of the *Parlement,* we find new appropriateness in the words '*as yet*' in the formel's statement:

> I wol noght serven Venus ne Cupyde
> For sothe as yet, by no manere wey (652–53).

Marie was born February 26, 1371,[22] and was beginning her seventh year at the time of these negotiations. Even the celebration of the royal nuptials, accordingly, would have carried with it a delay in the consummation of the marriage. On the other hand, Anne of Bohemia was born on May 11, 1366, and was therefore within a few months of her sixteenth birthday at the time of her marriage to Richard.

Finally, the negotiations for Anne's marriage seem to have been left in the hands of a group distinctly outside Chaucer's circle. Miss Rickert has already called attention to the fact that these negotiations were not entrusted, as would be expected, to John of Gaunt but

[22] According to the 'Table des Nativités' as quoted by L. Delisle (*Recherches sur la Librairie de Charles V,* I, 268–69) the year of Marie's birth is 1370, but this is Old Style reckoning. Anselme (*Hist. généalogique,* I, 110D) erroneously gives the date as 'le 27 février.' In this study, I have given the dates uniformly according to the New Style. For questionable calendar dates (326 A.D. to 1600 A.D.) see the rubric 'Pâques' in L. Lalanne's *Dictionnaire Historique de la France.*

to his younger brother, the Earl of Cambridge. Moreover, the marriage of Richard and Anne was determined largely through the intervention of papal politics; for after the Great Schism, Pope Urban, unfavorably inclined toward English affiliation with the supporters of his rival Pope Clement of Avignon, accomplished one of his objectives in promoting the English and German alliance.

CHAPTER V

The Dissension Among the Birds

TEN stanzas in the *Parlement of Foules* (lines 414–83) are devoted to presenting the claims of the three suitors. Then follows an episode of greater length (lines 484–616) in which the attention of the reader is diverted almost wholly from the rivalry of the suitors to the controversy between the 'fouls of ravyne' and the 'worm-fouls,' 'water-fouls,' and 'seed-fouls.' On this section of the poem, commentators have bestowed comparatively little attention; nor have they suggested any reason why Chaucer should have introduced this digression in the midst of the story of the rival tercels further than to remark that it was probably intended as a satire on current political affairs.

Miss Rickert has come closer than any one else, it seems to me, to Chaucer's purpose in this part of his allegory, which she aptly designates 'a bird House of Commons.'[1] The 'fouls of ravyne,' she says, represent the nobility, the 'water-fouls' the merchants, the 'seed-fouls' the country gentry, and the 'worm-fouls' the citizenry. Professor Emerson,[2] who was endeavoring to support his view of the date of the poem, had previously suggested in a footnote that Chaucer was here referring to the Parliament at Northampton which met in November, 1380. At all events he was certain

[1] *Mod. Phil.*, XVIII, p. 5.

[2] *Mod. Lang. Notes*, XXVI, p. 111, n. 10.

that the satire is directed at the anti-Lancastrian Commons.

Chaucer, it will be noted, represents the birds as conducting their controversy in accordance with Parliamentary procedure. Each of the factions chooses a spokesman to present its case and agrees to follow his leadership. And for employing birds in a political allegory there was precedent in actual contemporary politics. In the parliament of 1371 a nobleman described the church as an owl protected by the feathers which other birds (i.e., the baronage) had contributed.

But if Chaucer's allegory was designed as a covert allusion to contemporary events he would be most likely to turn for his material to the 'Good Parliament'[3] of 1376. In this epoch-making Parliament were assembled for the first time representatives of all social classes. The purposes of convening this Parliament, as stated by Sir John Knyvet, the Chancellor, were (1) to provide for the good government of the kingdom, (2) to prepare defenses from foreign enemies by land and sea, and (3) to carry on the war against France.[4] In point of fact, it was summoned on account of the strained relations which existed between members of the 'House of Commons' and executives of the King's council. The discussions of the convening groups were distinguished by extraordinary outspokenness on the part of the commons in the charges which they levelled against the favorites of the King.

Among the members of the royalist faction who were conspicuous targets for attack in the Good Parliament

[3] The Parliament of 1376 is called the Good Parliament because of the acts then passed. Compare the 'Bad Parliament' of 1377, so-called for its rejection of these acts.

[4] W. Longman, *Life and Times of Edward III,* II, p. 247.

were John of Gaunt, Alice Perrers, William Lord Latimer, and Sir Richard Stury—all of whom have been noted in Chapter II as persons with whom Chaucer was more or less directly associated. And from the point of view of this faction, at least, we may be certain that this Parliament was regarded as a turbulent and disorderly body.

In accordance with the avowed policy of correcting the evil practices of the King's favorites to insure better government, members of the Good Parliament petitioned for the removal of Alice Perrers and informed the King against her.[5] They stated that she was the wife of William de Windsor, the King's deputy in Ireland.[6] Edward appeared surprised to hear this report, swearing that he knew nothing of it; but he nevertheless requested that Alice be dealt with gently. The Commons, however, proceeded with their purpose, and under a general ordinance, which forbade women to practise in the courts of law, Alice was sentenced to banishment and forfeiture.[7]

Complaints were also brought against other members of John of Gaunt's clique. William Lord Latimer[8]

[5] Cf. 'Alice Perrers,' *Dict. Nat. Biog.*

[6] *Chronicon Angliae* (ed. E. Maunde Thompson), pp. 100, 104.

[7] Her property, which she is said to have acquired by unlawful means, was confiscated. Cf. *Dict. Nat. Biog.* Cf. Armitage-Smith, *John of Gaunt,* pp. 128ff.

[8] Armitage-Smith (*ibid.,* 128) says that though Latimer was occasionally employed by Gaunt, he 'was not of the Lancastrian party.' A contemporary chronicler (*Arch.,* XXII, 242) states that Alice induced Edward to favor him. Although Latimer may have led something of an independent career, his remarkable favor at court seems to have been due to the influence of Alice, with whom he was more than once associated in the latter years of Edward's reign.

was accused of unlawfully removing staple from Calais and of levying higher duties on merchandise than was authorized by Parliament. Prices were set so high and Latimer and his accomplices 'made such a great scarcity in this land of things saleable, that the common sort of people could scantily live.'[9] Although Latimer held such offices as Chamberlain and Privy Counsellor, which testify to his favor at court, his political connections did not avail him in the present extremity. The several charges made against him were proved, and he was forced to go to prison. This was the first record of an impeachment of a minister of the crown by the Commons.[10]

The conduct of the war also came in for criticism. Sir Peter de la Mare remarked that an excessive amount was being spent on war and that the negotiations for peace were accomplishing little. This charge was directed against John of Gaunt,[11] whose power at court saved him from stronger censure.

Some of the other favorites of the King were treated with less consideration. Sir Richard Stury, who acted as agent between Edward III and Parliament, was accused of making false and malicious reports concerning the intentions of the Commons.[12] Along with Lord Latimer he was thrown into prison.[13] Richard Lyons [14]

[9] Longman, *op. cit.*, p. 251. Cf. *Rot. Parl.*, 50 Edw. III, 17.

[10] *Dict. Nat. Biog.* s.v. Latimer.

[11] Armitage-Smith, *op. cit.*, pp. 142ff.

[12] T. Amyot, *Arch.*, XXII, 226. Cf. *Chron. Angliae*, 87, 89.

[13] Amyot, *ibid.*, 232.

[14] Lyons, who was favored by Alice Perrers (*Rolls of Parl.*, III, 12b–14a; *Chron. Angliae*, 136–38), was beheaded by Wat Tyler, whose master he had been, in the Peasants Rebellion of 1381 (Morant, *Hist. and Ant. of Essex*, II, 320). Latimer prob-

was also questioned, found guilty of illegal extortion of money, and sentenced to imprisonment. Sir John Neville, William Ellis, and John Peachy were other members of this circle to suffer loss of office and imprisonment. According to Longman, these were 'the boldest assertions of the right of the people to control the actions of the Government that had ever taken place in English history.'[15]

Even the King was not exempt from criticism. The Commons protested that the kingdom's riches were going to the private advantage of court favorites. The several complaints registered against the sale of corn and yarn were rejected by the King; but the only subsidy which Parliament would grant for the continuation of the war, equipment of ambassadors, and construction of defences was to renew (for another three years) the same subsidy on wool, etc., as had been granted three years before.[16]

The popular party in the Good Parliament received its most powerful support from the Black Prince, but he was already greatly weakened in health, and with his death on June 8 they lost their champion. It is said that the effect of the Parliament died with him.[17] On July 6, in any event, Parliament was dismissed.

But though the heated controversies of the Good Parliament may have supplied the suggestion for Chau-

---

ably lost his life in the same manner in 1381 (*Dict. Nat. Biog.*). Stury was in France at this time. Cf. Rymer, *Foedera,* VII, 308f. Waugh (*Scottish Hist. Rev.,* XI, 60) says 'luckily perhaps for himself (Stury) was in France treating for peace at the time of the Peasants' Rebellion.'

[15] *Op. cit.,* 254.

[16] *Ibid.,* 249–50.

[17] Longman, *op. cit.,* 246. Cf. Murimuth (ed. T. Hogg), p. 220.

cer's account of the discussions among the birds, it must not be forgotten that his poem was written not in 1376 but in 1377. During the intervening months the political situation had been reversed, and the royalist faction restored to power.

In January, 1377, the Bad Parliament convened. Young Richard, heir to the throne, opened the session in person. Thomas Hungerford, Speaker, secured a formal pardon for those who had been previously condemned; and Alice Perrers, Richard Stury, William Ellis, and others returned to court favor.[18] By the intervention of John of Gaunt, Lord Latimer had been released on bail May 26, 1376,[19] and by the restoration of his friends to power in 1377 he was able to reenter his old employments. In the spring of 1377 we find John of Gaunt, Alice Perrers, and their clique again holding political ascendancy.[20] They resume their old practices. Commissioners again receive assignments to go abroad to negotiate with France. Sir Peter de la

[18] *Ibid.*, 276–77.

[19] Cf. 'Latimer,' *Dict. Nat. Biog.*

[20] The relationship of members of this faction should not be confused. Alice's position at court is said to have induced John of Gaunt, Lord Latimer, and others to seek her favor in the last years of Edward's reign. Cf. *Dict. Nat. Biog.* In May, 1373, the Duke presented her with a handsome gift. Cf. Armitage-Smith, *John of Gaunt's Register,* No. 1343, p. 194. After Edward's death and Alice's consequent fall from prosperity, the Duke obtained a considerable amount of her property, including her hostel on the banks of the Thames. The Duke appears to have been openly opposed to Alice at this time. Cf. *Notes and Queries,* 7 S, VIII, pp. 97–98, 449–51. It was perhaps he who made it profitable for Stury to give evidence against her at the Parliament in the autumn of 1377. Waugh (*Scottish Hist. Rev.,* XI, 66) takes the point of view that Stury's testimony was made 'probably under compulsion.'

Mare, who had led the Commons in its attack on the royal party, was summoned to appear at court, where Alice Perrers joined with Stury and Latimer in securing his disgrace.[21]

If Chaucer was introducing the story of the bird-parliament for satirical purposes, he must have been aiming at some such dissension among social classes as characterized the Good Parliament. The tone of Chaucer's satire, one feels, is good-humored, not resentful or apprehensive. And such a tone would have suited perfectly with the political situation when Chaucer was engaged in his negotiations for the marriage of Richard and Princess Marie. What would be more natural than that he should have taken the opportunity to introduce into his poem satire on the opponents of his friends?

Notice particularly the characteristics of these classes as illustrated by their spokesmen. The 'fool cukkow,' representing the 'worm-foul,' puts himself forward officiously.

> I wol of myn owne auctorite
> For comune spede take the charge now (506–07).

And a little later the cuckoo shows that he cares only for his personal security and is indifferent to everything else:

> 'So I,' quod he, 'may have my make in pees
> I recche not how longe that ye stryve
> Let ech of hem be soleyn al hir lyve' (605–07).

This selfish indifference is sharply rebuked by the 'merlioun'—one of the 'fouls of ravyne':

> 'Ye! have the glotoun fild ynogh his paunche
> Then are we wel . . .
> Go, lewed be thou, whyl the world may dure' (610–16).

[21] Cf. 'Alice Perrers,' *Dict. Nat. Biog.*

Nor do the 'water-foul' display themselves to better advantage. The goose makes a bad impression at the outset by his self-importance and conceit:

> Pees! now tak kepe every man
> And herkeneth which a reson I shal bringe;
> My wit is sharp, I love no taryinge (563–65).

The advice of the goose is as profound as might have been expected from such a source.

> But she wol love him, lat him love another (567).

It is, in fact, as the 'sperhawk'—another of the 'fouls of ravyne'—remarks sarcastically, 'a parfit reson of a goos.'

Another representative of the 'water-foul,' the 'doke,' intrudes himself into the discussion with no less unfortunate results. The 'turtel trewe,' spokesman of the 'seed-foul,' has praised constancy in love:

> For thogh she deyed, I wolde non other make
> I wol ben hires, til that the deth me take (587–88).

But this fine spirit of fidelity means nothing to the 'doke,' who scoffs:

> There been mo sterres, god wot, than a paire (595).

For this cynical observation the 'doke' is silenced by the 'tercelet of the faucon'—another of the 'fouls of ravyne':

> Out of the dunghil com that word ful right (597).

Toward the 'worm-foul' and 'water-foul' Chaucer shows a scornful, even contemptuous, attitude. He displays them as ignorant, churlish, and bumptious (554–56). And in every instance, they are 'taken down' by some one of the birds of 'ravyne.' Toward the 'seed-foul' as represented by the 'turtel' his attitude is much more sympathetic. The 'turtel' expresses himself with becoming modesty ('and wex for shame al reed'); he dissents from the counsel of the goose, but without resorting to invective. If the 'seed-foul' represented the country gentry, it is clear that Chaucer regarded them in a very different light from the merchants and the Commons.[22] But it is equally clear that he gave allegiance in fullest measure to the 'fouls of ravyne,'[23] who represented the royalist faction in the parliamentary controversies of 1376 and 1377. Throughout they take precedence over the other orders, and the sentiments which they express are in every instance those which the poet himself approves.

Moreover, their spokesman, the 'tercelet of the faucon,' Chaucer seems to have intended as something more than a lay figure. The 'fouls of ravyne' choose him 'by pleyn eleccioun . . . to diffyne Al hir sentence, and as him list, termyne.' They then present him to Dame Nature 'And she accepteth him with glad entente.' The 'tercelet of the faucon,' furthermore, addresses himself directly to the three suitors, speaking with authority:

> Oure is the voys that have the charge in honde,
> And to the Iuges dome ye moten stonde (545–46).

He is also the only one of the spokesmen who really reviews the case of the rival suitors and by his con-

[22] By the 'water-foul' Chaucer seems to have been thinking of the little merchants who protested against the arbitrary fixing of prices by Latimer and his group.

[23] David Patrick (*Phil. Quarterly,* IX, 61–65) is surely incorrect in thinking Chaucer is critical of the 'fouls of ravyne.'

cluding words he seems to imply that he is confident as to the formel's ultimate decision:

> And of these three she wot hir-self, I trowe,
> Which that he be, for hit is light to knowe (552–53).

One will not fail to observe, further, that he is treated with peculiar deference by Dame Nature. Twice she quotes his words, and in both cases with high approval.

> For sith hit may not here discussed be
> Who loveth hir best, *as seide the tercelet* (624–25).
> [I] conseyle yow the ryal tercel take,
> *As seyde the tercelet ful skylfully* (633–34).

We shall probably not be mistaken, therefore, in supposing that Chaucer in the 'tercelet of the faucon' was describing a real person; and, of course, one to whom the royalist faction would naturally have turned as their leader. And if this supposition is correct, the only person who would have fitted such a rôle was manifestly John of Gaunt, Duke of Lancaster, who being the son of the aged King might appropriately have been described as 'the tercelet of the faucon.' Moreover, at the Parliament of 1376 John of Gaunt actually presided as the deputy of the King.[24]

Also, this identification would enable us to understand more clearly the statement of the tercelet on his appointment as spokesman. It is a difficult matter, he seems to say, to settle the choice among the suitors by public debate, for every one talks so much [25] that no one may be

[24] Cf. N. B. Lewis, *Eng. Hist. Rev.*, XLII, 404.

[25] Chaucer's word is 'replicacioun,' which in English as in Old French was used in the sense of repetition. Cf. *Orologium Sapientie* (*ca.* 1425), ed. C. Horstmann, *Anglia,* x, 342/12. Cf. Godefroy, *Lexique de l'Ancien Français.*

convinced by reason. He cannot see that arguments accomplish anything; accordingly it would seem 'ther moste be batayle.'[26] At this point he was interrupted by the over-eager suitors, but he had not finished his speech, and he resumes:

> It may noght gon, as ye wolde, in this weye;
> *Oure is the voys that han the charge in honde,*
> And to the Iuges dome ye moten stonde (544–46).

The 'tercelet' appears to be expressing his distaste for the noisy clamor of the parliamentary discussions.[27] This question is one which must be decided by a responsible body. Is it not likely that he is here referring to the deliberations of the commissioners who had been appointed to consider the peace treaty and the marriage negotiations, in the direction of which, as is well known, John of Gaunt was closely concerned?

It may be objected that this interpretation of the poem does not remove all inconsistencies. Why should the choice between the suitors be discussed by the assembled birds if the decision did not rest with them? The obvious reply is that these inconsistencies are not created by this interpretation but are inherent in the allegory itself. But no one will demand strict consistency of the mediæval allegorist. Chaucer in dealing with the marriage negotiations under the guise of a Valentine Day assembly of birds was following established literary convention. But he saw opportunity to

[26] Clearly he is not thinking of a resort to military operations but rather of the courtly institution of trial by combat. The suitors, at least, understand his words in this sense.

[27] Chaucer in a slightly earlier passage had devoted two stanzas (vv. 491–504) to satirizing the noisy debates of the birds.

bring into his picture satirical observations on contemporary political affairs by adding the allusions to the stormy debates of the Good Parliament. In this he deviated from his literary models and did violence to his allegory, but as a result he created a far livelier and more original poem.

CHAPTER VI

THE 'PARLEMENT OF FOULES' CONSIDERED IN ITS LITERARY RELATIONSHIPS

IT remains to consider how the *Parlement of Foules,* with the date 1377 established by the occasion for its composition, fits into the Chaucerian chronology. In discussing this question we shall need to examine the poem in its relation to Chaucer's other works.

The structure of the *Parlement,* as has long been recognized,[1] is loosely connected. The poem falls naturally into two parts, one from line 1 to 371 and the other from line 371 to the end. Commentators have observed that in the *Parlement,* as in the *Book of the Duchess,* Chaucer still shows an inability to lead up to his theme directly. In fact, it is not until we come to his abrupt 'But to the poynt' (line 371) that he really touches the main subject of his narrative, which, as Professor Root has well said, 'constitutes the real substance of the poem . . . [and] is, so far as we know, Chaucer's own original production.' [2]

In the first part, Chaucer does little more than weave together material which he took from older books. We may list briefly the sources from which this earlier portion was compiled.

From the Classics Chaucer derived a great deal for the beginning of the poem. He drew upon Cicero's *Somnium Scipionis,* which he found in the commentary

[1] Skeat, *Minor Poems,* p. 67.

[2] R. K. Root, *The Poetry of Chaucer,* p. 66.

of Macrobius, for the episode of his suggestive dream.[3] Ovid also seems to have provided him with a few details in these opening lines.[4] Ovidian material is likewise indicated as a probable source for three of the lovers in the poet's famous list;[5] namely, Candace, Scylla, and Rhea Silvia.[6] Professor Shannon[7] further proposes that Chaucer knew Ovid's *Fasti* as the poet called Priapus a god and the Latin form of his name is used. Claudian's *In Sextum Consulatum Honorii Agusti Praefatio* (3–10) is fairly closely translated by the poet in the fifteenth stanza of the *Parlement*.[8] All together the classics make up a considerable contribution in forming a subsidiary framework for the more significant allegory of the birds.

Among mediæval sources the first used by Chaucer is Alanus de Insulis, whom he mentions by name.

> And right as Aleyn, in the Pleynt of Kinde,
> Devyseth Nature of aray and face (316–17).

In the *De Planctu Naturae* the birds are represented merely as part of the embroidery upon the robe of the

[3] Skeat, *Minor Poems*, 67ff. Professor Sypherd (*Studies in Chaucer's Hous of Fame*, 23–25 and notes) believes Skeat overstates this influence. Professor Shannon (*Chaucer and the Roman Poets*, 13ff.) compares *P. F.*, 10–13 with Ovid's *Amores*, I, 9; *Ars Am.*, I, 9; and *Remedia Amoris*, 1–40. R. D. French (*Chaucer Handbook*, 94) considers Chaucer's synopsis to be contained in *P. F.*, 36–84.

[4] E. F. Shannon, *ibid.*

[5] *P. F.*, 288–94.

[6] Shannon, *ibid.* Skeat (*op. cit.* in notes) referred to Livy and the *Æneid* for Rhea Silvia.

[7] *Chaucer and the Roman Poets*, 14ff.

[8] Cf. R. D. French, *A Chaucer Handbook*, p. 95. Moreover, in Claudian there is a dwelling to which the adventurous Cupid repairs. Cf. Neilson, *Court of Love*, p. 15.

goddess, so that from this source Chaucer took hardly more than a suggestion, and a few names of the birds, for his literary purposes.[9] To another Latin writer, Joseph of Exeter, Chaucer seem to owe some of the epithets employed in his quaint descriptions of the tree list in lines 176–82.[10]

The extensive field of mediæval French literature afforded Chaucer occasional suggestions. It has been suggested that Chaucer may have found the title for his poem in Marie de France's fable, *Li Parlemens des oiseaux pour faire Roi.*[11] There are also many French love-visions which would afford him suggestions.[12] For example, the general setting of the *Parlement of Foules* bears some resemblance to Jean de Condé's *La Messe des Oisseaus.*[13] Birds are also associated with Venus in the *Roman de la Rose.*[14] But Chaucer's poem is more like French love-vision poetry in tone than in achieved effect. The Birds' Matins,[15] Cupid and his arrows,[16] and other descriptive passages are purely conventional.

[9] *De Planctu Naturae* may be consulted in T. Wright's *Anglo-Latin Satirical Poets,* II, 437ff. Cf. D. M. Moffat's English translation in *Yale Studies in English,* XXXVI. Cf. Skeat, *Minor Poems,* 73–74.

[10] Cf. R. K. Root, 'Chaucer's Dares,' *Mod. Phil.,* XV, 18ff.

[11] Cf. Skeat, *op. cit.,* p. 75. Legouis (*Geoffrey Chaucer,* p. 82) seems to be incorrect in believing a 'part of the poem' was suggested to Chaucer by Marie's fable. Cf. French, *op. cit.,* p. 94.

[12] Neilson, *Court of Love,* pp. 24ff., 42ff.

[13] Sypherd, *op. cit.,* p. 24.

[14] Neilson, *op. cit.,* pp. 8ff.

[15] *Ibid.,* pp. 216–28.

[16] *Ibid.,* 39ff. Cf. Miss E. P. Hammond's (*M. L. N.,* XXXI, p. 121) ingenious suggestion regarding *P. F.,* line 214.

For the *rondeau* with which Chaucer concludes his story of the birds, Furnivall [17] referred to Machault and Monoit de Paris. Chaucer introduces the 'roundel' as follows:

> The note, I trowe, maked was in Fraunce;
> The words were swich as ye may heer finde,
> The next vers, as I now have in minde (677–79).

The line immediately following which reads 'Qui bien aime a tard oublie' appears to be a proverb.[18]

Finally, by way of summary, the *Parlement,* like the *Book of the Duchess* and *Hous of Fame,* is substantially French in style, particularly because it contains the usual personages of the goddess Venus, the attendant Cupid, and an important guide; and also because it employs such conventional descriptions as the colorful temple of Venus, the personifications of Delight, Youth, Flattery, and the like, and the dream- and vision-motive in which birds play a part. Some characteristics of Chaucer's earlier poetry, itself French in atmosphere, persist in the *Parlement,* as we see on comparing it with the *Duchess* or the *Compleynt unto Pite,* a poem also written in *rime royal.* When Chaucer discovers that 'Pite' has died, he finds gathered 'About hir herse,'

> Withouten any wo, as thoughte me,
> Bountee parfit, wel armed and richely,

[17] *Trial-Forewords,* pp. 55–56.

[18] I find 'Qui bien aime tar oblie' included as a proverb in U. Robert's 'Recueil d'Anciens Proverbes,' *Bibl. de l'École des Chartes,* XXXIV, 33–46. Cognate forms of this proverb are 'Qui bien aime envis haist' and 'Qui bien aime bein chastie.' Ernest Langlois, 'Anciens Proverbes Français,' *Bibliothèque de l'École des Chartes,* LX, Nos. 592, 595, p. 593.

And fresshe Beaute, Lust, and Jolitee,
Assured Maner, Youthe, and Honestee,
Wisdom, Estaat, (and) Dreed, and
Governaunce (*Pite,* 36–41).

And in the *Parlement* Chaucer 'was war' of a similar company:

I saw Beautee, withouten any atyr,
And youthe, ful of game and Iolyte,
Fool-hardinesse, Flatery, and Desyr,
Messagerye, and Mede, and other three—
Hir names shul noght here be told for me—(*P. F.,* 225–29).

But the entering wedge of Italian sources marks an advancement in narrative technique beyond this earlier poetry; for in the *Parlement* we have what may be the earliest appearance of Italian influence in Chaucer's work. Boccaccio's *Teseide*[19] provides Chaucer with sixteen stanzas of picturesque description, which decorative passages form some of the most attractive elements of this poem rich in color and significance. And Dante's *Inferno,* as Furnivall and Skeat have noted, also contributes a suggestion for a few lines.[20] Moreover, Professor Lowes[21] finds that the poetic enumeration of famous lovers in Stanza XLII of the *Parlement* is really a fusion from Chaucer's reading in both Boccaccio and Dante. In Boccaccio's list Chaucer read about 'Della sposa di Nin,' 'Piramo e Tisbe,' 'Ercole,' and 'Bibli'; in Dante's catalogue he found: 'Nino, e fu sua sposa,' 'Semiramis,' 'Cleopatras,' 'Elena,' and

[19] See Skeat (*Minor Poems,* 68–73) for the Italian text and William Rossetti's translation.

[20] Cf. Furnivall, *Trial-Forewords,* pp. 75ff. See also Skeat's notes to *P. F.* in *Minor Poems.*

[21] *Mod. Phil.,* XIV, 705–35.

'Achille.' Chaucer's stanza may be read in the light of these names:

> Semyramus, Candace, and Ercules,
> Biblis, Dido, Tisbe and Piramus,
> Tristram, Isoude, Paris, and Achilles,
> Eleyne, Cleopatre, and Troilus,
> Silla, and eek the moder of Romulus—
> Alle these were peynted on that other syde,
> And al hir love, and in what plyte they dyde (288–94).

But this list of famous lovers and 'many a mayde,' though one of the most colorful adornments of Chaucer's love-vision setting, is not unusual as a poetic device. Gower sees, in *Confessio Amantis* (III, 357ff.), Cupid's glorious company: Tristram and Isolde, Lancelot and Gunnor, Galahat and his lady, Jason and Creusa, and some others.

In contrast to the Classical, French and Latin sources, the Italian material incorporated into the poem, though perhaps more considerable in extent, is less significant as motive for the narrative. A greater reliance upon and better integration of Italian material is evident in the *Hous of Fame;* but in the *Parlement* the influence of Italian literature, which seems to be confined to Boccaccio's *Teseide* [22] and Dante's *Inferno,*[23] consists merely in adding incidental decoration.

[22] Koeppel's suggestion (*Anglia,* XIV, pp. 233–36) that Chaucer borrowed certain lines from Boccaccio's *Amorosa Visione* in writing the *Parlement* is doubtful.

[23] Lowes (*Mod. Phil.,* XIV, p. 132f.) claims an instance (*P. F.,* 139–56) of Chaucer's indebtedness to Dante's *Paradiso* (IV, 1–12). Whatever be the case for the *Parlement,* Chaucer seems to have been very well acquainted with the Italian language. Cf. S. B. Meech, *P. M. L. A.,* XLV, 128. That the poet knew Italians in England is not unlikely. Cf. Edith Rickert, *L. T. L. S.* (Oct. 4, 1928), p. 707.

Indeed, the *Parlement* shows in every respect the characteristics of what Professor Kittredge calls the Transition Period; that is, from 1373 down to the *Palamon and Arcite*. In the *Parlement* there is, to summarize our review, the old classical material, Ovid and the *Somnium Scipionis,* the pervasive tone and atmosphere of French love-vision poetry, and the new Italian influence of Boccaccio and Dante. Professor Kittredge has himself well remarked upon the qualities of Chaucer's work at this stage of his artistic development:

> We may expect, then, in case there are any poems in the Chaucer canon that meet our expectations for the Transition Period, that, while not prevailingly Italian, they will contain passages from Dante.[24]

In the essay referred to, Kittredge[25] enumerates the pieces belonging to this period, the *Life of St. Cecilia,* the *Monk's Tale,* and the *Hous of Fame.* He probably did not feel free to include the *Parlement of Foules* on account of the general acceptance of Koch's date for the poem. Nevertheless, its character conforms perfectly, it will be observed, to the definition which he gives.

Are there still other poems which might reasonably be assigned to this period? The points of contact between the *Parlement* and *Compleynt of Mars* justify the inference that these poems belong to the same period of composition. The 'Proem' of Chaucer's *Mars* opens with an injunction to the birds and proceeds to name the season of their convention.

[24] *The Date of Chaucer's Troilus,* p. 40.
[25] *Ibid.,* pp. 40ff.

'Gladeth, ye foules, of the morow gray,
Lo! Venus risen among yon rowes rede!
And floures fresshe, honoureth ye this day;
For when the sonne uprist, then wol ye sprede.
But ye lovers, that lye in any drede,
Fleeth, lest wikked tonges yow espye;
Lo! yond the sonne, the candel of jelosye!' (*Mars,* 1–7.)
(Seynt Valentyne! a foul thus herde I singe
Upon thy day, er sonne gan up-springe). (*Mars,* 13–14.)

Concerning the *Compleynt of Mars* we have the important testimony of Shirley [26] that it was written about 'my lady of York doughter to the kyng of Spaygne and my lord of Huntyngdoun some tyme duc of Excestre . . . ,' and the composition of this poem may, therefore, be assigned to a date in the neighborhood of 1374. Scholars are not in agreement as to the meaning or chronology of the *Mars;* [27] but the appearance of the St. Valentine's day device and the usual wandering narrative characteristic of Chaucer's early manner seem to indicate that this poem preceded the *Parlement.*

The date of *Anelida and Arcite* has not been fixed with any certainty, but since it uses a good deal of the

[26] Shirley's note was appended to his copy of the *Compleynt* in a manuscript preserved in the library of Trinity College, Cambridge.

[27] S. H. Cowling (*Rev. Eng. Studies,* II, 405–10, and *Chaucer,* pp. 60ff.) and Brusendorff (*Chaucer Tradition,* pp. 265ff.) do not improve on Shirley's testimony, and both writers encounter an objection in dating the poem 1386. The *Compleynt of Venus* may be, as Shirley said and these writers seem to believe, an answer to the *Mars,* but it was undoubtedly written some years later. C. R. Baskervill (*P. M. L. A.,* XXXVI, 565–614) believes the *Mars* to be a conventional subject diversified by an astronomical allegory.

Teseide material, and undoubtedly preceded the *Palamon,* we may regard it as near in date to the *Parlement.* It is quite likely, too, that the *Compleynt to his Lady,* in which the *terza rima* appears and from which a number of lines passed a little later into the *Anelida and Arcite,* belongs to the early years of the Transition Period.

Scholars have not reached any clear decision as to the relative priority of the *Hous of Fame* and the *Parlement,* although Professor Kittredge unhesitatingly assigns the *Fame* to the Transition Period. With the date of the *Parlement* moved back to 1377, it becomes more probable that it preceded the *Hous of Fame.*[28] It will be noticed that the influence of Dante is more pervasive and extensive in the *Fame.*[29]

No confusion is introduced into the Chaucerian chronology by the new dating of the *Parlement;* and, on the other hand, it offers certain manifest advantages. In the period of 1381–1385 we have to consider perhaps the *Hous of Fame,* certainly *Palamon and Arcite,* and the beginning of work on *Troilus and Cressida* could hardly have been postponed later than 1382. Chaucer's translation of Boethius, since it was very likely written before *Troilus,* also belongs here. A long tract from Boethius is introduced into *Troilus,* and in his *Words*

[28] Professor Carleton Brown (*P. M. L. A.,* XXVI, 6–30) has noted that the *shul* and *shal* forms in the two poems would favor the priority of *P. F.*

[29] It may be added that while the influence of *Amorosa Visione* on *P. F.* is doubtful, scholars agree that this work of Boccaccio's influenced *H. F.* Cf. Koeppel (*Anglia,* XIV, 233–38) and Child (*M. L. N.,* X, 379, 84). Cf. Tatlock, *Development and Chronology,* 40 and note 1.

unto Adam Chaucer mentions Troilus and 'Boece' together. The otherwise rather crowded period of 1381–85 is relieved by the earlier date of 1377 for the *Parlement.* It is, in fact, a satisfaction to have another poem which can definitely be placed before Chaucer's second journey to Italy.

BIBLIOGRAPHY

Anselme, P., *Histoire généalogique et chronologique de la Maison Royale de France,* Vol. I (third edition), Paris, 1726.

Anquetil, M., *Histoire de France,* Vol. v, Paris, 1829.

Amyot, Thomas, 'An Historical Relation of certain passages about the end of King Edward the Third, and of his Death,' *Archæologia,* XXII (Society of Antiquaries of London, 1829), pp. 204–84.

Armitage-Smith, Sydney, *John of Gaunt, King of Castile and Leon, Duke of Aquitaine and Lancaster, Earl of Derby, Lincoln and Leicester, Seneschal of England,* Westminster, 1904.

Armitage-Smith, Sydney, *John of Gaunt's Register* (Camden Historical Society, Third Series), London, 1911.

Astronomical Papers, VI, pt. III, Washington, 1895.

Barante, M. de, *Histoire des Ducs de Bourgogne,* Vol. IV, Paris, 1839.

Baskervill, C. R., 'English Songs of the Night Visit,' *Publications of the Modern Language Association,* XXXVI (1921), 565–614.

Beaven, Alfred B., 'The Grocers' Company and the Aldermen of London in the Time of Richard II,' *English Historical Review,* XXII (1907), pp. 523–25.

Biographie Universelle, Vols. VIII, XII, Paris, 1884.

Braddy, Haldeen, 'The *Parlement of Foules:* A New Proposal,' *Publications of the Modern Language Association,* XLVI (1931), pp. 1007–19.

Brown, Carleton, '*Shul* and *Shal* in the Chaucer Manuscripts,' *Publications of the Modern Language Association,* XXVI (1911), pp. 6–30.

Brusendorff, Aage, *The Chaucer Tradition,* London, 1925.

Buchon, J. C. L., *Les Chroniques de Jean Froissart,* Vol. VI, Paris, 1867.

Calendar of Patent Rolls (Public Record Office).

Calendar of Close Rolls (Public Record Office).

Calendar of Papal Registers: Papal Letters, IV (Public Record Office).

Child, C. G., 'Chaucer's *House of Fame* and Boccaccio's *Amorosa Visione,*' *Modern Language Notes,* X (1895), pp. 379–84.

Christine (de Pisan), *Le Livre des Fais et bonnes meurs du sage roy Charles,* V (in Col. d. mém.; ed. Petitot, v. 5), Paris, 1819.

Clement-Simon, G., *La Rupture du Traité de Brétigny et ses conséquences en Limousin* (1368–1377), Paris, 1898.

Collinson, Rev. John, *The History and Antiquities of Somerset,* Vols. III, London, 1791.

Cook, A. S., 'The Historical Background of Chaucer's Knight,' *Transactions of the Connecticut Academy of Arts and Sciences,* XX (1916), pp. 161–240.

Cosneau, E., *Les Grands Traités de la Guerre de Cent Ans* (Collection de Textes, v. VII), Paris, 1889.

Coulton, G. G., *Chaucer and His England,* New York, 1908.

Cowling, S. H., *Chaucer,* London, 1927.

Cowling, S. H., 'Chaucer's *Complaintes of Mars and of Venus,*' *Review of English Studies,* II (1926), 405–10.

Delachenal, R., *Chronique des Régnes de Jean II et de Charles V* (Soc. de l'Hist. de France, III Vols.), Paris, 1920.

Delaville le Roulx, J., *La France en Orient au XIVe Siècle* (Bibliothèque des Écoles Français d'Athénes et de Rome, No. 45), Paris, 1886.

Delisle, Leopold, *Mandements et Actes Divers de Charles V* (1364–1380) (Coll. de Doc. inédits, publié pour l'Instruccion Publique), Paris, 1874.

Delisle, Leopold, *Recherches sur la Librairie de Charles V,* Partie I, Paris, 1907.

Delisle, Leopold, *Le Cabinet des Manuscrits de la Bibliothèque Nationale,* Vol. III, Paris, 1881.

Déprez, Eugène, *Études de Diplomatique Anglaises,* Paris, 1908.

Devillers, Léopold, *Cartulaire des Comtes de Hainaut,* Vols. II and VI, Bruxelles, 1883.

Dictionary of National Biography, Vols. IV, XI, XII, XV, Oxford, 1921–22.

Dieudonné, H., 'La Monnaie Royale de Charles V à Charles VI,' *Bibliothèque de l'École des Chartes,* LXXII (1911), pp. 473–79.

Dodd, William George, *Courtly Love in Chaucer and Gower* (Harvard Studies in English, I), Boston, 1913.

Douglas, T. W., 'What is the Parlement of Foules?' *Modern Language Notes,* XLIII (1928), pp. 378–84.

La Grande Encyclopédie, Vol. X, Paris, n. d.

Emerson, O. F., 'The Suitors in Chaucer's *Parlement of Foules,*' *Modern Philology,* VIII (1910), pp. 45–62.

Emerson, O. F., 'The Suitors in the *Parlement of Foules* Again,' *Modern Language Notes,* XXVI (1911), pp. 109–11.

Emerson, O. F., 'What is the *Parlement of Foules?*' *Journal of English and Germanic Philology,* XIII (1914), pp. 566–82.

Emerson, O. F., 'Chaucer's First Military Service,' *Romanic Review,* III (1914), pp. 321–61.

Farnham, W. E., 'The Sources of Chaucer's *Parlement of Foules,*' *Publications of the Modern Language Association,* XXXII (1917), pp. 492–518.

Farnham, W. E., 'The Fowls in Chaucer's *Parlement,*' *University of Wisconsin Studies in Language and Literature,* No. 2 (1918), pp. 341ff.

Farnham, W. E., 'The Contending Lovers,' *Publications of the Modern Language Association,* XXXV (1920), pp. 247–323.

Fleay, F. G., *Guide to Chaucer and Spenser* (Collins' School and College Classics), London and Glasgow, 1877.

Furnivall, F. J., *Trial Forewords to my Parallel-Text Edition of Chaucer's Minor Poems* (Chaucer Society Publications), London, 1871.

Gilliodts-Van Severen, L., *Le Cotton Manuscrit Galba B. I.* (Académie Royale des Sciences et des Beaux-Arts de Belgique), Bruxelles, 1896.

Godefroy, F., *Lexique de l'Ancien Français,* Paris and Leipzig, 1901.

Hammond, Eleanor P., 'Chaucer and Dante and Their Scribes,' *Modern Language Notes,* XXXI (1916), p. 121.

Hammond, Eleanor P., '*Chaucer, A Bibliographical Manual,*' New York, 1908.

Hasted, *History of Kent.* Part I, *The Hundred of Blackheath* (ed. H. H. Drake), London, 1886.

'Hermentrude,' *Notes and Queries,* 7 Series, VIII, pp. 97–98; pp. 449–51.

Hœpffner, Ernest, *Œuvres de Guillaume de Machaut* (Société des Anciens Textes Français), Paris, 1911.

Horstmann, C., 'Orologium Sapientiae or The Seven Poyntes of Trewe Wisdom, aus MS. Douce 114,' *Anglia, Zeitschrift für Englische Philologie,* X (1888), pp. 323–89.

Hulbert, James Root, *Chaucer's Official Life* (Dissertation, the University of Chicago), Menasha, Wisconsin, 1912.

'Jeo voile Droict,' *Notes and Queries,* 7 Series, VIII, pp. 30–31.

Kervyn de Lettenhove, *Œuvres de Froissart,* Vols. VIII and XXIII, Brussels, 1869, 1877.

Kirk, R. E. G., *Life-Records of Chaucer,* IV (Chaucer Society, Publications), London, 1900.

Kittredge, G. L., 'Chaucer and Froissart,' *Englische Studien,* XXVI (1899), pp. 321–36.

Kittredge, G. L., 'Chaucer and Some of His Friends,' *Modern Philology,* I (1903), pp. 1–18.

Kittredge, G. L., *The Date of Chaucer's 'Troilus' and Other Chaucer Matters* (Chaucer Society, Publications), London, 1909.

Koch, John, *The Date and Personages of the 'Parlament of Foules,' Essays on Chaucer,* IV (Chaucer Society, Publications), London, 1877.

Koch, John, 'Ein Beitrag zur Kritik Chaucer's,' *Englische Studien,* I (1877), pp. 249–93.

Koch, John, *The Chronology of Chaucer's Writings* (Chaucer Society, Publications), London, 1890.

Koch, John, 'Alte Chaucerprobleme und Neue Lösungsversuche,' *Englische Studien,* LV (1921), pp. 161–225.

Koeppel, E., 'Chauceriana: Boccaccio's *Amorosa Visione,*' *Anglia, Zeitschrift für Englische Philologie,* XIV (1892), pp. 233–36.

Kuhl, E. P., 'Index to *The Life-Records* of Chaucer,' *Modern Philology,* X (1913), pp. 527–52.

Labarte, Jules, *Inventaire du Mobilier de Charles V* (Coll. de Docs. inédits), Paris, 1879.

Lalanne, L., *Dictionnaire Historique de la France,* IV Vols., Paris, 1872.

Lalanne, L., *Œuvres Complètes de Brantôme,* Vol. VIII: 'Les Dames' (Soc. de l'Hist. de France), Paris, 1875.

Lange, Hugo, 'What is the Parlement of Foules? (Eine Chaucer-notiz),' *Anglia, Zeitschrift für Englische Philologie,* XL (1916), pp. 394–96.

Langhans, Viktor, *Untersuchungen zu Chaucer,* Halle, 1918.

Langlois, Ernest, 'Anciens Proverbes Français,' *Bibliothèque de l'École des Chartes,* LX (1899), pp. 569–601.

Lavisse, Ernest, *Histoire de France,* Vol. IV, Paris, 1902.

Lefévre, André, 'Apogée de Charles, V (1377–78),' *Revue de l'École d'Anthropologie de Paris,* XIII (1903), pp. 101–21.

Legouis, Emile, *Geoffrey Chaucer* (L. Lailavoix's English translation), New York, 1913.

Lewis, N. B., 'Article VIII of the Impeachment of Michael de la Pole in 1386,' *English Historical Review,* LXII (1927), pp. 402–07.

Litta, Pompeo, *Famiglie celebri l'Italia,* Florence, n. d.

Longman, William, *The Life and Times of Edward III,* Vol. II, London, 1869.

Lowes, J. L., 'Chaucer and Dante,' *Modern Philology,* XIV (1917), pp. 705–35.

Luce, Siméon, *Chronique des Quatre Prémiers Valois* (1327–1393) (Soc. de l'Hist. de France), Paris, 1862.

Luce, Siméon, and Gaston Raynaud, *Chroniques de J. Froissart,* Vol. VIII (Soc. de l'Hist. de France), Paris, 1888.

Macaulay, G. C., *The Complete Works of John Gower. The English Works,* Vol. III, Oxford, 1901.

Manly, J. M., 'What is the Parlement of Foules?' *Festschrift für Lorenz Morsbach. Studien zur Englische Philologie,* L (1913), pp. 279–90.

Manly, J. M., *Some New Light on Chaucer,* New York, 1926.

Martene, E., and U. Durand, *Thesaurus Anecdotorum,* Vol. I, Paris, 1717.

Mas-Latrie, L. de, 'Nouvelles Preuves de l'Histoire de Chypre,' *Bibliothèque de l'École des Chartes,* XXXIV (1873), pp. 84–86.

Meech, S. B., 'Chaucer and an Italian Translation of the *Heroides,*' *Publications of the Modern Language Association,* XLV (1930), 110–28.

Mirot and Dépréz, 'Les Ambassades Anglaises pendant la guerre de Cent Ans,' *Bibliothèque de l'École des Chartes,* LX (1899), pp. 177–214.

Moffat, Douglas M., *The Complaint of Nature* (Alain, de Lille) (Yale Studies in English, XXXVI), New York, 1908.

Moore, Samuel, 'A Further Note on the Suitors in the *Parliament of Fowls,*' *Modern Language Notes* (1911), pp. 8–12.

Moore, Samuel, 'New Life-Records of Chaucer,' *Modern Philology,* XVI (1918), pp. 49–52.

Moore, Samuel, 'New Life-Records of Chaucer—Addendum,' *Modern Philology,* XVIII (1922), pp. 497–98.

Morant, P., *History and Antiquities of Essex,* II Vols., London, 1768.

Moranvillé, R., *Chronographia Regum Francorum* (Soc. de l'Hist. de France), Paris, 1893.

Neilson, W. A., *The Origins and Sources of the 'Court of Love'* (Harvard Studies and Notes in Philology and Literature, VII), Boston, 1895.

Nicolas, Sir Nicholas Harry, *Testamenta Vetusta,* II Vols., London, 1826.

Nicolas, Sir Nicholas Harry, *Proceedings and Ordinances of the Privy Council of England,* Vol. I, London, 1834.

Nicolas, Sir Nicholas Harry, 'Memoir' to *The Poetical Works of Geoffrey Chaucer,* Vol. I (Aldine Edition), London, 1845.

Paris, Gaston, and Ulysse Robert, *Miracles de Nostre Dame,* Vol. VIII (Soc. des Anciens Textes Français), Paris, 1893.

Patrick, David, 'The Satire in Chaucer's *Parliament of Birds,' Philological Quarterly,* IX (1930), pp. 61–65.

Petitot, editor of *Les Mémoires de Du Guesclin* (Coll. Comp. des mém., IV, I Series), Paris, 1819.

Piaget, A., 'Oton de Granson et ses Poesies,' *Romania,* XIX (1890), pp. 237–39, 403–48.

Pollard, Alfred W., *Chaucer Primer,* London, 1895.

Reid, May E., 'The Historical Interpretations of the *Parlement of Foules,' University of Wisconsin Studies in Language and Literature,* No. 18 (1924), pp. 60–70.

Rickert, Edith, 'A New Interpretation of the *Parlement of Foules,' Modern Philology,* XVIII (1920), pp. 1–29.

Rickert, Edith, *London Times Literary Supplement* (October 4, 1928), p. 707.

Robert, Ulysse, 'Un Vocabulaire Latin-Francais du XIVe Siècle, suivi d'un Recueil d'Anciens Proverbes,' *Bibliothèque de l'École des Chartes,* XXXIV (1873), pp. 33–46.

Root, R. K., 'Chaucer's Dares,' *Modern Philology,* XV (1917), pp. 1–22.

Root, R. K., *The Poetry of Chaucer* (Revised Edition), Boston, 1922.

Root, R. K., and H. N. Russel, 'A Planetary Date for Chaucer's *Troilus,' Publications of the Modern Language Association,* XXXIX (1924), pp. 49–63.

Rymer, Thomas, *Foedera* (Record Edition), London, 1816–1831, 1869.

Secousse, H., *Histoire de Charles-le-Mauvais,* Vol. I, Paris, n. d.

Shannon, Edgar Finley, *Chaucer and the Roman Poets,* Harvard University Press, 1929.

Shears, F. S., *Froissart, Chronicler and Poet,* London, 1930.

Simonde de Sismondi, J. C. L., *Histoire des Français,* Vol. XI, Paris, 1828.

Skeat, W. W., *The Complete Works of Geoffrey Chaucer,* VI Vols., Oxford, 1894. *Chaucerian Pieces,* Vol. VII, Oxford, 1897.

Sypherd, W. O., *Studies in Chaucer's 'Hous of Fame'* (Chaucer Society, Publications), London, 1907.

Tatlock, J. S. P., *The Development and Chronology of Chaucer's Works* (Chaucer Society, Publications), London, 1907.

Thompson, E. Maunde, *Chronicon Angliae* (Chron. and Mem. of Great Britain. The Rolls Edition), London, 1874.

Tout, T. F., 'The Chief Officers of the King's Wardrobe down to 1399,' *English Historical Review,* XXIV (1909), pp. 496–505.

Warburton, Rev. W., *Edward III,* New York, 1895.

Ward, Sir A. W., *Chaucer* (English Men of Letters), London, 1875.

Walsingham, Thomas, *Historia Anglicana* (1272–1381, 1381–1422), II Vols. (Ed. H. T. Riley, Chron. and Mem. of Great Britain. The Rolls Edition), London, 1863–64.

Walsingham, Thomas, *Ypodigma Neustriae* (Ed. H. T. Riley, Chron. and Mem. of Great Britain. The Rolls Edition), London, 1876.

Waugh, W. T., 'The Lollard Knights,' *Scottish Historical Review,* XI (1913), pp. 55–92.

Wilkinson, B., 'A Letter to Louis de Male, Count of Flanders,' *Bulletin, The John Rylands Library, Manchester,* IX (1925), pp. 177–87.

Wright, Thomas, *The Anglo-Latin Satirical Poets and Epigrammatists of the Twelfth Century,* Vol. II (The Rolls Edition), London, 1872.

SUPPLEMENTARY BIBLIOGRAPHY

THE PROBLEM SINCE 1932

In the descriptive summary which follows, I have endeavored to review all the important publications on Chaucer's *Parlement* since the issuance of my interpretation in 1932. My survey covers thirty-five years, from 1932 through 1967, and comprises relevant items listed by Professor Albert C. Baugh in his Goldentree Bibliography entitled *Chaucer* (New York, 1968), pp. 35-37. The abbreviations used below are standard and may be found in either Baugh's listings, already noted, or the annual bibliography in *PMLA*.

Baker, Donald C. "The Poet of Love and the *Parlement of Foules*." *USME,* II (1961), 79-110. Reviews major theories of the past and holds that *PF* is later than *HF*.

Bennett, J. A. W. *The Parlement of Foules: An Interpretation.* Oxford: Clarendon Press, 1957. Discusses at length almost all aspects of the poem except historical interpretations like mine.

Bethurum, Dorothy. "The Center of the *Parlement of Foules*." *Essays in Honor of Walter Clyde Curry* (Nashville: Vanderbilt Univ. Press, 1954), pp. 39-50. Focuses on the Garden of Love and states that there is implied irony in Chaucer's concern for the "commune profit" and the absence of this sense in the avian parliament.

Braddy, Haldeen. "The Historical Background of the *Parlement of Foules*." *RES,* XI (1935), 204-209. Replies to objections raised by Manly.

Braddy, Haldeen. "Froissart's Account of Chaucer's Embassy in 1377." *RES,* XIV (1938), 1-5. Answers Manly's further objections by a defense of Froissart's accuracy.

Braddy, Haldeen. "Chaucer's Comic Valentine." *MLN,*

LXVIII (1953), 232-234. Asserts that Chaucer's complimentary poems may have comic overtones and yet contain serious allusions to real persons and actual events.

Brewer, D. S., ed., *The Parlement of Foules*. London: Nelson, 1960 (*Nelson's Medieval and Renais. Library*). Concerns aesthetic appreciation rather than historical interpretation.

Brewer, D. S. "The Genre of the *Parlement of Foules*." *MLR,* LIII (1958), 321-326. Regards Graunson's *Songe* as inferior to *PF* and wonders if Graunson did not borrow from Chaucer rather than vice versa.

Bronson, Bertrand H. "The *Parlement of Foules* Revisited." *ELH,* XV (1948), 247-260. Says Chaucer affirms that he is past the age for love and ready to undertake more serious matters.

Bronson, Bertrand H. *In Appreciation of Chaucer's Parlement of Foules*. Berkeley: 1935 (*Univ. of Calif., Pub. in English,* III, No. 5, 193-223). Holds that poetic merit is the special quality which gives *PF* its enduring value.

Damon, Phillip W. "The *Parlement of Foules* and the *Pavo*." *MLN,* LXVII (1952), 520-524. Lists ten alleged similarities between *PF* and the thirteenth-century Latin *Pavo,* poem by Jordanus of Osnabruck.

Emslie, Macdonald. "Codes of Love and Class Distinctions." *EIC,* V (1955), 1-17. Cf. *ibid.,* 405-407 (C. Clark), 407-413 (D. Brewer), 413-418 (Emslie); VI (1956), 248 (Brewer). Avows that different classes of men represent various ideals of amorous conduct.

Everett, Dorothy. "Chaucer's Love Visions with Particular Reference to the *Parlement of Foules*." *Essays on Middle English Literature,* ed. Patricia Kean (Oxford: Clarendon Press, 1955), pp. 97-114. Assumes the blended role of scholar and critic as she depicts Chaucer gaining a deeper insight into love from his search, yet unable to answer major questions about the relationship.

Frank, Robert W., Jr. "Structure and Meaning in the *Parlement of Foules.*" *PMLA,* LXXI (1956), 530-539. Sees unity in the three parts of *PF* with Chaucer poking fun at different views of love.

Friedman, William F. and Elizabeth S. "Acrostics, Anagrams, and Chaucer." *PQ,* XXXVIII (1959), 1-20. Attack Ethel Seaton's cryptology and contend that almost any number of names can be described by scrambling alphabetical letters.

Goffin, R. C. "Heaven and Earth in the 'Parlement of Foules'." *MLR,* XXI (1936), 493-499. Affirms that the poet is searching for heavenly bliss as opposed to the morality of poetry and attributes lofty concepts of love to the tercels as opposed to the earthy outlook of the humbler fowls.

Griffin, Mary. "The Pekok with His Aungels Fetheres Bryghte." *Studies on Chaucer and His Audience* (Quebec: 1956, for private distribution), pp. 49-66. Regards Chaucer's audience as a sophisticated one and distinguishes between the decorative peacock and the *Pavo* as a symbol of the pope.

Huppé, Bernard F., and D. W. Robertson, Jr. *Fruyt and Chaf: Studies in Chaucer's Allegories.* Princeton: Princeton Univ. Press, 1963. [*BD, PF*]. Deal with the philosophy and ideas in the poem, picture Chaucer finding wisdom to be the only real love, and define the mood throughout as ironic.

Lange, Hugo. "Hat Chaucer den Kompass Gekannt und Benutzt?" *Anglia,* LVIII (1934), 333-344. Believes that Chaucer was an expert on astronomy and describes a sea compass of Charles V of France.

Lange, Hugo. "Zu Chaucers *Vogelparlament.*" *Anglia,* LX (1936), 397-400. Dates *PF* as 1380 by magnetic compass and identifies the formel with either Catherine of France or Catarina of Milan.

Lange, H., and A. Nippoldt. "Die Deklination am 20. Mai 1380 in London." *Quellen und Studien zur Geschichte der Naturwissenschaften und der Medizin,* V, No. 4 (1936), 38-56. Speak of 1380 as the date of *PF* and discuss marriage negotiations featuring Richard and Catherine of France and later Richard and Anne of Germany.

Lange, Hugo. "Ein neuer Chauserfund: Zu John Kochs Richard-Anna-Theorie (Vogelparlament)." *ESt,* LXVIII (1933-34), 174-187. Analyzes heraldic evidence to identify the one-headed eagle with Richard II, accepts 1380 as the date of *PF,* and evaluates Catherine of France and Anne of Germany as prototypes of "even might."

Lange, Hugo. "Die Nordnordwest-Stellung der Venus und der Nordwestwind in Chaucers *Vogelparlament.*" *Anglia,* LXIV (1940), 196-204. Seeks to show that Chaucer used a magnetic rather than an astronomical measurement, says the power of the star of love is broken and asserts that a northwest wind was accepted as a friendly omen for journeying from Dover to Calais.

Lumiansky, Robert M. "Chaucer's *Parlement of Foules*: A Philosophical Interpretation." *RES,* XXIV (1948), 81-89. Finds Chaucer's theme to be a treatment of true and false felicity.

Malone, Kemp. "Chaucer's Daughter of Cupid." *MLR,* XLV (1950), 63. Accepts "Wille" as her current name, l. 214.

Manly, John M. "Mr. Braddy and the *Parlement of Foules.*" *RES,* X (1934), 267-273. Launches objections to Braddy's theories largely by questioning his methods of research and the validity of Froissart's reporting the betrothal for 1377.

Manly, John M. "Correspondence." *RES*, XI (1935), 211-213. Restates his objections to Braddy's first rejoinder *(RES*, XI (1935), 204-209) but later ignores Braddy's second *(ibid.*, XIV (1938), 1-5).

Manzlaoui, Mahmoud. "Ars Longa, Vita Brevis." *EIC*, XII (1962), 221-224. Says Chaucer shows poetic tact in his opening lines and a confusion of meaning in his closing ones.

McDonald, Charles O. "An Interpretation of Chaucer's *Parlement of Foules*." *Speculum*, XXX (1955), 444-457. Asserts that Chaucer deals with various ideas of love, especially true and false conceptions.

Moore, Arthur K. " 'Somer' and 'Lenten' as Terms for Spring." *N&Q*, CXCIV (1949), 82-83. States that in the sixteenth century "spring" came into use as a word for the space between equinox and solstice, that by "somer" Chaucer therefore means "spring," and that at about the end of the thirteenth century "somer" replaced "lenten."

Owen, Charles A., Jr. "The Role of the Narrator in the *Parlement of Foules*." *CE*, XIV (1953), 264-269. Thinks the poet assumes a naive personality as narrator and that the poem itself has topical, critical, and allegorical meanings.

Perry, Thomas E. "Chaucer's *Parlement of Foules*: Man in the Medieval Universe." (M. A. Thesis, University of Virginia, 1967. Pp. 1-38). Explains that Chaucer's *somnium* was a very special kind of dream that conceals something incapable of being understood except by interpretation; claims also that the poem deals with "the failures of distinct persons within the noble class to provide for the well-being of the realm" (p. 33). [See The Poet's Continental Interests in the new Introduction].

Pratt, Robert A. "Chaucer Borrowing from Himself." *MLQ*, VII (1946), 259-264. Cites arresting and crucial instances of Chaucer's borrowings either from his sources or from himself and believes these data may be used to date one composition as earlier or later than another.

Pratt, Robert A. "Chaucer's Use of the *Teseida.*" *PMLA,* LXII (1947), 598-621. Holds that Chaucer used Dante's *Commedia* only a little more than Boccaccio's *Teseida* as major Italian sources for his English works.

Raymo, R. R. "The *Parlement of Foules* 309-15." *MLN,* LXXI (1956), 159-160. Argues that the source here is *Speculum Stultorum,* by twelfth-century Nigel de Longchamps.

Rowland, Beryl. "Chaucer's 'Throstil Old' and Other Birds." *MS,* XXIV (1962), 381-384. Adds learned notes on such birds as "throstil" (364), "feldefare" (364), "fesaunt" (357), and "swan" (342).

Samuel, Irene. "Semiramis in the Middle Ages: the History of a Legend." *M&H,* II (1944), 32-44. Offers pagan (good) and Christian (evil) views of Semiramis in commenting on *PF* (270-294).

Seaton, Ethel. "The *Parlement of Foules* and Lionel of Clarence." *MAE,* XXV (1956), 168-174. Cf. *ibid.,* XXVI (1957), 107-109 (K. T. Emerson); 109-111 (Seaton). See also: Friedman, William F. and Elizabeth S. "Acrostics, Anagrams, and Chaucer." *PQ,* XXXVIII (1959), 1-20. Attempts to find acrostic anagrams to link *PF* with Lionel, Violanta, and Galeazzo as the principal figures in a marriage poem; but other commentators manipulate the evidence to come up with yet other historical names.

Selvin, Rhoda H. "Shades of Love in the *Parlement of Foules.*" *SN,* XXXVII (1965), 146-160. Suggests that in treating different types of love Chaucer favors spiritual devotion and deplores courtly *amour.*

Slaughter, E. E. " 'Every Vertu at his Reste.' " *MLN,* XLVI (1931), 448-453. Affirms that "every" (376) refers to the courtly virtues and "at his reste" to "in its home", the formel thus becoming the embodiment of all worthwhile attributes.

Smith, Roland M. "Five Notes on Chaucer and Froissart." *MLN,* LXVI (1951), 27-32. Treats in Note Three several allusions to Candace, including one in *PF,* as borrowed from Froissart's *L'Espinette* (1. 1798) and as referring to an Indian Queen of that name.

Stillwell, Gardiner. "Unity and Comedy in the *Parlement of Foules.*" *JEGP,* XLIX (1950), 470-495. Regards Chaucer's tone throughout as ironic, finds Graunson's *Songe* to be serious, and concludes that even the bird lovers in the assembly are comic.

Stillwell, Gardiner. "Chaucer's Eagles and Their Choice on February 14." *JEGP,* LIII (1954), 546-561. Compares Chaucer's treatments with those of Graunson, Gower, Lydgate, and Charles of Orleans; and holds that *PF* is a kind of parody of courtly love.

Wilhelm, James J. "The Narrator and His Narrative in Chaucer's *Parlement,*" *ChauR,* I (1967), 201-206. Sees the poem as divided into three parts: The Dream of Scipio, the Love Vision, and the World of Reality (where Nature presides); interprets the narrator as the gentle observer of life who only "seeks" knowledge of love; and maintains (rightly, I believe) that Nature is the true "heroine" of the *Parlement.*